Diet to Lose Weight

Lose Weight Fast with DASH Diet Recipes and Grain Free Goodness

Adrienne Simmons and Kristina Harper

Table of Contents

t

YOUR GRAIN FREE MEAL PLAN

Introduction

How fast you actually lose weight is determined upon several different things. First, your body build and the amount of weight you need to lose. Second, your willingness to follow through and stick with the diet plan. Third, your physical activity (exercise) or lack thereof will all determine just how fast you will lose weight. To make a diet successful you must prepare in advance for dieting. Just stopping what you are doing (eating lots of junk food, being sedentary) will not work as well as it would if you work up to it. Most importantly you mental attitude toward the diet and your body is a big determining factor in success.

When you go on a diet to lose weight you need to realize why you got that way in the first place. Chances are you are overweight due to two factors factor one - you enjoy too much junk food and do not eat enough nutritious food and factor two - you are too sedentary. When you consider what these two factors do to your health then you must realize it takes more than just going on a diet to fix it. Sure, you can go on a diet to lose weight and lose the weight. But unless you make permanent changes the weight will come right back once you stop dieting. So do not look at dieting as a temporary fix. Make a determination to make it a permanent change, a complete change of lifestyle. Once you do this then your chance of successful weight loss goes way up and you will be able to maintain the weight loss as well. Success depends on what you do to prepare for the weight loss.

Fast weight loss is relevant. If you can lose a good amount of weight within a 3 to 6 month time frame then you are doing good, this is a healthy fast weight loss plan. Any faster and the diet will not be healthy, unless you only need to lose 10 pounds, then in that case you can probably lose it within a month. So be reasonable when you approach this. If you are serious about weight loss and want it to work right then you will make the steps necessary to get there.

The first thing you should do before you start the diet is to realize that junk food is a severe addiction. It is as severe as smoking cigarettes. Break the addiction before you start the diet so you will be able to go on the diet and this will prompt the weight loss. Breaking a bad habit or any habit takes about three weeks to make it a success. The body and the mind needs this time to readjust. But first understand what food addiction does to you and why it's so bad.

Carbs, specifically from junk food, is highly addictive. It is mostly sugar. Sugar sticks with the body and turns into fat. The more you eat the more you want. The more you eat the more you crave it. The more you eat the less it satisfies you. Perhaps you have noticed if you eat a snack of junk food, you may have a boost of energy followed by a crash. This boost of energy is false because it is not sustaining. It is a bad cycle because many think that the short burst of energy is good and will repeat eating the snack just for the boost.

Contrary to eating junk food, nutritious food does not do this. You will not eat something nutritious only to have a false boost of energy followed by a crash. Quite the opposite, eating nutritious food will give you a good boost of energy that will sustain you. Nutritious food will also aid an overweight body into burning the fat and thus losing the weight. In order to get to that point wean yourself from the junk food first.

Keep a journal of the foods you eat, how often and the portions. Next, you will want to divide the amount of junk food you consume into replacing one food every several days. You do this by replacing one junk food; for example, say you eat a candy bar every afternoon. Start there and replace it with something nutritious, say an apple, or a few nuts. Continue eating as you normally do except for that one time for three or four days. Then replace another instance of consuming junk food with a nutritious food item. Keep doing this until you have successfully replaced all the junk food with healthier food. This will give your body a chance to overcome the junk food addiction without the unpleasant side effects of weaning such as headache, food cravings, moodiness, and extreme hunger.

Add Exercise

If you add exercise to your healthy lifestyle change, you will do so much better than if you don't. Part of the reason for obesity is lack of exercise. Perhaps you lead a busy life and don't have time to hit the gym. Whatever the reason it will benefit you greatly if you take some time to add an exercise routine to your weekly schedule. All it takes to make a difference is to be physically active for at least half an hour every other day. That's it. The exercise needs to help you break a sweat. A brisk walk where you are moving your arms is much better than a leisurely walk with your hands shoved in your pockets. Make it even better by adding a ten-minute warm up and cool down before and after the work out. This can be simple stretches, stretching the arms, legs, abdomen, and back. The key to successful and fast weight loss is the addition of physical activity to the diets.

Disclaimer

Everything listed in this book is for informational purposes only. It is advisable to seek the advice and counsel of your health care provider before starting any new diet or exercise routine.

Section 1: DASH Diet

The DASH Diet is an important strategy for anyone who wants to lower their blood pressure and improve their overall health without dealing with risky medications and their side effects. This simple diet focuses on low fat, low cholesterol foods and natural ingredients, making it inexpensive and easy to follow. Plus, you'll be surprised by how delicious heart healthy foods can be. If you've been warned about the possible dangers of high blood pressure and a normal North American diet, it's time to make some changes.

The recipes contained in this book don't encompass the entire range of DASH diet options, but they will give you an idea of how you can change your favorite foods to fit the diet plan. In general, they focus on reducing the fat, cholesterol and refined carbohydrates in a dish without losing out on flavor. If you've experienced too many flavorless health foods, these recipes could be the solution that you've been hoping for.

What Is the DASH Diet?

DASH is a term that stands for "Dietary Approaches to Stop Hypertension." It is designed to be a lifestyle change for people who want to treat or prevent hypertension, also known as high blood pressure. The diet is based on studies originally performed by the US National Institutes of Health that examined three different dietary plans and their effects on blood pressure. The result is a plan that focuses on increased consumption of plant foods such as nuts, beans, low fat dairy products, vegetables and fruit.

This diet plan is recommended by the National Heart, Lung and Blood Institute for anyone who wants to decrease their blood pressure and improve heart health. In studies performed on the diet, people who followed it showed a systolic blood pressure reduction of 6mm Hg, as well as a diastolic blood pressure reduction of 3 mm Hg in patients who had tested in the high-normal range, also called pre-hypertension. In patients who had existing hypertension, the diet caused reductions of 11 mm Hg and 6 mm Hg respectively, with no change in body weight. While it was not designed for weight loss, the DASH diet's focus on lower calorie, healthier foods does make it a viable choice for people who want to reduce their body fat levels.

What Is Hypertension and Why Is It Dangerous?

Hypertension, or high blood pressure, refers to the force your blood puts on the walls of your arteries. Doctors measure it in millimeters of mercury, or mm Hg, and record it as two different numbers. They measure both the systolic blood pressure, or the pressure when your heart is beating, and the diastolic blood pressure, or the pressure between beats. A person's blood pressure can rise and fall over the course of a given day, but continued high levels can be very dangerous to your health.

When your blood flows with a lot of force, it can damage the veins and arteries, as well as organs like the eyes, heart, kidneys and brain. Most people who develop high blood pressure have difficulty lowering it. Left uncontrolled, this condition can lead to blindness, kidney and heart disease, and even stroke. About one in three people have high blood pressure, but many aren't aware of the problem.

Many doctors and patients turn to medication at the

first sign of high blood pressure, but this technique might not be the right one for you. Many blood pressure treatments have dehydrating effects. Others can induce depression or extreme tiredness. The very low blood pressure that is caused by some drugs can also result in severe dizziness and a tingling feeling in your fingers and toes. In more serious cases, these drugs can cause insomnia, pain in the feet, weakness and leg cramps, or an irregular heartbeat. That's a lot of risk to take when you could address the problem through less intrusive methods like diet and exercise.

How Does the DASH Diet Work?

The DASH diet provides an alternative to conventional, drug-based methods of controlling blood pressure. It is designed to help you maintain a healthy weight with moderate levels of physical activity. It focuses on reducing sodium levels, which have been shown to elevate blood pressure in some people. It also includes decreased levels of saturated fat and cholesterol, which contribute to narrowing of the arteries and can make it hard for blood to cycle properly.

Over time, this diet can help patients who have high blood pressure lower their levels and reduce their medication requirements. In some cases, it can even allow you to discontinue use of medication entirely. It is important to change your dosages only on the recommendation of a doctor, however. Don't stop using your high blood pressure medicine just because you've started using the DASH diet.

DASH Study Daily Nutrient Goals

The studies used to formulate the DASH diet set a few standard daily nutrient goals, which are also used in the main plan. Following this diet means trying to keep your total fat intake to about 27 percent of your daily calories. Saturated fat should make up only about 6 percent of your calories, however. The DASH diet is relatively high in carbohydrates, which should make up about 55 percent of your daily calorie intake, but most of the carbohydrates you eat should be complex ones, rather than those derived from white flour and sugar.

The DASH diet also recommends trying to keep your daily cholesterol intake below 150 milligrams. The original studies aimed for a sodium intake of 2,300 milligrams or less, but more recent research suggests that 1,500 milligrams or less is even better for reducing blood pressure. It's a good idea to get at least 30 g of fiber and 1,250 milligrams of calcium each day while on this diet, as well.

DASH Diet Guidelines

All those number can be hard to understand, so the researchers who wrote the DASH diet plan broke it down into clearer recommendations. They suggest eating six to eight servings of whole grain per day, four to five servings of vegetables, and four to five servings of fruit. Consuming two to three servings of low fat dairy products provides protein and calcium. If you eat meat, aim to consume six or fewer one-ounce servings of lean meat, poultry or fish per day. Vegetarians can substitute an egg for one serving of meat.

The DASH diet guidelines recommend consuming four to five servings of nuts, legumes and seeds per week, though vegetarians should increase these to replace meat. Fats and oils should be kept to a relative minimum of two to three servings per day. This includes, mayonnaise, margarine and salad dressings. Sweets need to be eaten in moderation; the DASH diet recommends having five low-fat servings or fewer every week. Very active people can increase servings of grain, fruits and vegetables, low fat dairy and lean meat to help support their higher metabolisms.

Using DASH for Weight Loss

The DASH diet wasn't originally designed to help people lose weight, but it can be adapted to help you maintain a healthier weight and reduce your risk of high blood pressure. Doctors recommend simply using the lower calorie recommendations for the diet to cut back your energy intake. Eat a little less than you normally would and focus on getting about 30 to 60 minutes of regular physical activity, like walking or swimming, every day. Your weight may not decrease dramatically, but it should drop slowly over a longer period of time. Experts recommend this kind of loss because it is the most likely to be permanent.

Intuitive Eating with the DASH Diet

While many people like to start out counting their calories to ensure they're getting the right level of nutrition on the DASH diet, this doesn't work for everyone. If you have trouble with calorie counting, or if you've been on the diet long enough to know your choices are good ones, it might be time to look at intuitive eating. This technique involves paying attention to the signals your body is sending. When you've mastered intuitive eating, you'll provide food when your body is hungry, stop eating when it sends signals of fullness, and avoid snacking for emotional reasons or out of boredom. This method can be very helpful for people who tend to have trouble with more mathematical techniques, but it does take some practice.

Intuitive eating is compatible with the DASH diet from the beginning, but you'll need to modify your strategy a little bit. Start out by focusing on the low calorie foods that are acceptable on this diet. That means consuming more fruit and raw, non-starchy vegetables while eating more calorically-dense foods in small amounts. Even if you have a craving for nuts, beef or cheese, try having just a few bites to begin with. You may be able to conquer your craving quickly without overeating.

Making DASH Dieting Easy

The transition period between a normal North American diet and the DASH technique can be a rocky one, especially if you don't know how to find tasty snacks or eat at your favorite restaurants. Make things simpler by keeping pre-cut fresh fruit, vegetables and low-calorie dairy snacks in your refrigerator at all times. That way, when you want to grab something simple, they'll be right at your fingertips.

Make eating out on the DASH diet easier by turning the menu into a treasure hunt. You may be surprised by how many healthy foods you can find. Most restaurants now offer a veggie burger instead of a beef burger. You may also be able to choose steamed vegetables or fresh fruit rather than French fries or onion rings. Choose a garden salad with a light oil and vinegar dressing in restaurants that don't offer many vegetable options, and be sure to take part of your meal home. You'll find eating out on the DASH diet much simpler than you expected.

Last, but not least, practice sneaking DASH foods into your ordinary meals. It's easy to add cucumber slices, shredded cabbage or carrots to an ordinary sandwich. If you usually consume tea or coffee, add a full glass of skim milk to it to boost protein without increasing your cholesterol. Vegetable broths and fruit purees provide a great way to ensure you're getting all your fruits and veggies: just drink them!

Exercise and the DASH Diet

The DASH diet works well on its own, but when paired with exercise, it has considerably better effects. In one study of 124 men and women over the age of 50, 30 minutes of aerobic exercise three times per week lower blood pressure and weight much more quickly than diet alone. If you need to make lifestyle changes in order to improve your blood pressure and reduce your BMI, adding light to moderate physical activity is the best way to do it.

The process is very simple. Just add a half hour of swimming, walking or other activity to your day at least three times per week. The workout doesn't need to be severe. In fact, you should be able to hold a conversation while you're getting your exercise. Try to recruit a workout buddy to help keep you on track and develop healthy habits. You'll soon be feeling lighter and more energetic. You'll even develop more stamina, making it easier to stay active.

Recipes for the DASH Diet

These recipes are adapted from books and online sources. They range from very simple to multi-step preparations for fancier occasions, but you don't have to be a master chef to prepare them. While several of them rely on slightly unusual ingredients, you should be able to find these at many standard grocery stores. Consider checking the ethnic or natural foods section for low-sodium soy sauce, chili paste and other less common ingredients. The extra flavor they give to your meals makes it worthwhile to seek these foods out.

You don't have to jump straight into preparing just DASH diet recipes, either. You can incorporate a few of these dishes into your normal routine, increasing them until you're eating healthy all week long. That's what makes the DASH diet such a good idea. It helps you make healthy decisions and incorporate them into your life without having to turn your normal way of eating upside down. If you care about the health of your heart, arteries and brain, it may be time to try out some of these great DASH recipes. In just a little while, you won't know how you ever lived without them.

Appetizers

DASH Spinach Dip

This cheesy dip eliminates the cholesterol-laden cream cheese and full-fat sour cream normally used in spinach dips, substituting velvety Great Northern beans and low fat dairy. Instead of heavily-salted ingredients, it relies on flavorful herbs and garlic to add interest. The result is a creamy dip that doesn't taste like health food. It makes a great choice for parties and goes well with sliced vegetables or warm, crusty bread.

Ingredients

2 pounds fresh spinach or 3 packages frozen spinach
1 pound or one can cooked Great Northern beans
½ cup low fat sour cream
2 tablespoons Parmesan cheese
2 tablespoons fresh parsley
1 tablespoon fresh basil
2 teaspoons black pepper
2 cloves fresh garlic

Wash and drain the fresh spinach or thaw and drain if you are using frozen products. Drain the beans and mash or puree until smooth. Combine all ingredients and stir until well combined, then pour into an oven-safe dish. Bake at 350 degrees Fahrenheit for about 30 minutes or until the mixture is hot throughout and bubbly.

Stuffed Portabella Mushrooms

Stuffed mushrooms are a classic appetizer, but they too-frequently contain cholesterol-packed bacon, cream cheese, eggs and other health-hazard ingredients. This version uses fresh spinach combined with garlic, tarragon and strongly-flavored cheese to provide excitement without the fat. The make-ahead element of these stuffed mushrooms means they're the perfect last-minute choice when you have company or just don't want to spend too much time in the kitchen

Ingredients

4 large portabella mushrooms
1 cup fresh or frozen spinach
4 teaspoons grated Parmesan cheese
1 tablespoon fresh tarragon
2 teaspoons olive oil
2 cloves fresh garlic
½ teaspoon black pepper

Crush the garlic and remove the stems from the portabella mushrooms. Chop the stems finely. Drain the spinach thoroughly. Heat 1 teaspoon of olive oil over medium-high heat in a heavy pan and sauté the garlic, pepper and tarragon for one minute. Add the mushroom stems and spinach leaves to the pan, sautéing 3 to 4 minutes or until stems are tender. Remove and place in a bowl. Add remaining 1 teaspoon of olive oil to the pan and place the mushrooms in the pan, cap-side down. Saute for 3 minutes without stirring or turning.

Flip the caps, cover, and reduce heat to low for another 2 minutes. Remove and place the caps on a foil-lined baking sheet with the gills facing up. Fill each mushroom with ¼ of the spinach mixture. Top with Parmesan cheese. If you are making the recipe ahead, cover the sheet with plastic wrap and place it in the refrigerator or freezer until ready to serve. Otherwise, place the mushrooms on a rack 6 inches below your broiler and cook for 3 to 4 minutes, until the cheese has just browned.

Crispy Coconut Chicken Fingers

Coconut shrimp is a perennial favorite, but it's also loaded with saturated fat and cholesterol. This healthier alternative uses chicken thighs to offer just as much flavor in a better-for-you package. Combined with the sweet and spicy dipping sauce, this recipe will be a hit at your next party. Vegetarians and vegans can also enjoy this dish; just substitute tempeh for the chicken and egg replacement powder for the egg white as preferred.

Ingredients

½ pound boneless, skinless chicken thighs
¼ cup no-sodium bread crumbs
¼ cup unsweetened coconut flakes
1 teaspoon powdered garlic
1 egg white
¼ teaspoon black pepper
Dipping Sauce
2 tablespoons orange marmalade
1 ½ teaspoons rice vinegar or lemon juice
¼ teaspoon cayenne pepper

Wash the chicken and pat it dry. Slice into 20 individual bite-sized pieces. Combine the bread crumbs, coconut, garlic and black pepper in a small bowl. Beat egg white thoroughly. Dip each piece of chicken into the egg, then roll in the bread crumb mixture. Place on a lightly-oiled baking sheet and bake at 425 degrees for 10 minutes. Flip each piece, then return the sheet to the oven for another 10 minutes.

Combine all sauce ingredients in a small bowl and stir to combine. Arrange the chicken bites on a platter around the bowl of sauce and serve right away.

Vegetable Sushi

When you mention sushi, most people assume raw fish or eggs will be involved, but the term "sushi" actually refers to the slightly sour rice. You can top this delicate Japanese food with all kinds of ingredients, including fresh and colorful vegetables. Use brown rice to add more fiber and a nutty flavor. You can mix and match the vegetables in this recipe, making it an excellent choice to use up leftovers.

Ingredients

1 cup short grain brown rice
1 1/2 cups water
1 tablespoon plain rice vinegar
1 package sushi nori seaweed sheets
Vegetables
steamed or roasted asparagus spears
avocado
roasted beets
fresh cucumber strips
pickled daikon or radish
shredded kale
roasted sweet potatoes
roasted kale
fresh or sautéed mushrooms

thin slices of tomato

Place the brown rice in a pan or rice cooker brown and rinse until the water runs clear. Drain and add 1 ½ cups of water. Cook until the rice is tender. Sprinkle with vinegar and add salt substitute to taste. Stir with a wide, flat spoon or a rice paddle and allow the mixture to cool.

To assemble, place one sheet of nori on a bamboo sushi mat. Spoon approximately ½ cup of the cooked rice mixture in a thin layer across the whole piece of nori. Place shredded kale, asparagus stalks, cucumber strips or other vegetables on top of the rice, then roll the seaweed over the vegetables and into a long log, using the mat to keep it intact. Place the finished roll seam-side-down on a cutting board and slice into pieces with a very sharp knife. Serve immediately with pickled ginger, low sodium soy sauce, horseradish or sesame seeds.

Fresh Mushroom Quesadillas

Mushroom quesadillas are a popular dish in Mexico, where they are referred to as quesadillas de hongo. Unlike processed American versions of Hispanic cuisine, this dish is light and healthy without being dull or flavorless. Say goodbye to fatty, uniform Mexican fast food and hello to healthy flavor with these spicy but savory tortillas.

Ingredients

1 pound fresh mushrooms

1 medium onion

1 cup shredded Swiss cheese

¼ cup low fat sour cream

3 cloves garlic

2 tablespoons fresh cilantro

1 fresh jalapeno pepper

1 teaspoon olive oil

1 package low sodium, whole grain flour or corn tortillas

Finely chop mushrooms, onion, jalapeno, cilantro and garlic. Heat 1 teaspoon of olive oil in a heavy pan over medium heat and sauté the alliums and mushrooms for about 10 minutes, or until tender and lightly browned. Season with black pepper to taste. Heat a large skillet to medium-low and place a single tortilla on the surface, flipping to warm throughout. Sprinkle with cheese, chopped jalapeno and cilantro. Allow the cheese to melt, then spoon on a small amount of the mushroom mixture. Add a second tortilla and flip the entire quesadilla over. Remove to a plate to cool and repeat until you have used all the cheese and mushroom mixture. Slice each quesadilla into quarters or eighths, depending on the size of your tortilla. Serve warm with low fat sour cream.

Beverages

Peanut Butter and Banana Smoothie

Whether you'd like to enjoy a smoothie for breakfast, dessert or a between-meal treat, this one is a great choice. The banana provides plenty of natural sweetness, while the peanut butter offers monounsaturated "healthy" fats and protein. Combined with non-fat milk, this could be the perfect pick me up when you're feeling tired. Vegans can substitute unsweetened soy or almond milk.

Ingredients

1 cup skim milk
1 medium banana
1 tablespoon creamy natural peanut butter, unsalted

Peel and slice the banana. Place in a blender or food processor and add the milk and peanut butter. Process until completely smooth. For a more milkshake-like version, freeze the banana before blending.

No-Booze Margarita

Most people on the DASH diet need to take alcohol in moderation, while some need to eschew it completely. This tasty beverage offers the same overall flavor as a margarita, but without the alcohol. That means you can drink it at any time!

Ingredients

2 cups ice
½ cup lime juice
2 tablespoons simple syrup
Sliced limes for garnish
Simple Syrup (makes 6 tablespoons):
¼ cup raw sugar
¼ cup water

Combine the water and sugar in a small saucepan over medium heat, stirring until the sugar has dissolved completely. Remove to a sealed container and refrigerate for up to a week.

Combine syrup, ice and lime juice in a blender or powerful food processor. Process until a smooth slush has formed. Pour into a chilled glass and garnish with lime slices.

Sugar-free Agua Fresca

Aguas fresca, sweet non-carbonated beverages popular in Mexico and the southeastern US, can be a refreshing choice for hot days. Unfortunately, most of these drinks contain large quantities of white refined sugar. This variation uses fresh fruit to provide the sweetness, making it a much healthier and lower-calorie option you can enjoy more often.

Ingredients

3 pounds watermelon
½ cup unsweetened cranberry juice
½ cup apple juice
¼ cup lime juice
1 lime

Remove the seeds and rind from the watermelon, cutting it into fine dice. Place it in a food processor or blender and process until a smooth puree is produced. Sieve this puree to remove the excess pulp, yielding a clear, delicious juice. Cut the lime into thin slices. In a large pitcher, combine the watermelon juice, cranberry juice, apple juice and lime juice. Stir to combine completely. The mixture may be slightly cloudy, but it will taste delicious when refrigerated and garnished with a slice of fresh lime.

Spicy, Sweet and Tangy Herbal Tea

Technically a tisane, because no tea leaves are involved in its brewing, this drink can be served either warm or chilled. It uses only natural, unprocessed sweeteners, making it an excellent alternative to sodas and conventional iced tea beverages.

Ingredients

1 ½ quarts water
½ cup fresh mint
1/3 cup lemon juice
3/8 cup strongly-flavored honey
4 tablespoons fresh ginger
1 medium lemon

Peel and chop the ginger. Slice the lemon thinly into rounds. Combine the ginger, water and lemon juice in a saucepan and bring to a boil over high heat. Reduce to low and allow to simmer for 5 minutes. Add the mint, remove from heat entirely, and allow to steep for 5 to 8 minutes. Use a fine sieve to remove the mint leaves and ginger, which can be discarded after use. Stir in the honey and serve warm or cold with a lemon slice floating on top.

Non-Alcoholic Hurricane Punch

Traditionally made with rum, this beverage is a great choice to add lots of vitamin C and other antioxidants to your diet. When made with ice, it becomes a delicious frosty drink that's perfect for a hot summer day.

Ingredients

2 cups or 1 can fresh unsweetened pineapple

1 orange

1 lemon

1 lime

½ cup unsweetened cranberry juice

1 cup ice (optional)

Peel the citrus fruit and set aside. Chop the pineapple roughly into chunks and combine in a blender with the cranberry juice and citrus. Add the ice if you are using it and process until the mixture is a smooth liquid or frosty puree. Serve in tall glasses with a spoon for the icy version.

Breakfast

Chewy Fruit Bars

This simple bar is sweet and hearty, making it the perfect choice for breakfast on the go. Unlike many ordinary granola bars, it's not high in fats or refined sugars, however. Natural ingredients such as multigrain cereal and bran help keep the glycemic index low, while walnuts, dried fruit and almond butter provide the energy your body needs to keep going. Enjoy these bars as a quick snack or even a light dessert in a pinch.

2 cups dry whole grain hot cereal
1 cup bran flakes cereal
¾ cup honey
¾ cup low salt almond butter
½ cup non-fat dry milk
½ cup dried apricot pieces
½ cup dried cranberries
½ cup walnut pieces
1 tablespoon canola or light olive oil
1 tablespoon vanilla extract

In a large bowl, combine cereals, nuts, dried fruit and dry milk. Place almond butter, honey and oil in a small saucepan and heat to medium-low, stirring constantly. Allow mixture to bubble, then remove the pan from the heat and add vanilla extract. Pour this mixture over the fruit and cereal, stirring until completely combined. Grease a baking pan with canola oil or line it with parchment paper. Spread the mixture into the pan, patting it down tightly. Bake for 20 minutes at 325 degrees and set aside to cool on a rack for 20 minutes or until firm. Cut into 12 pieces and store in an air-tight container at room temperature.

Broiled Almond-Banana Toast

Bananas are a classic breakfast ingredient, but on their own they tend to be carbohydrate-heavy and unsatisfying. That's why this morning treat pairs fresh banana with fiber-rich whole grain toast and protein-packed almond butter. Putting the finished product under the broiler caramelizes the natural sugars in the banana, producing a delicious, gooey result that you'll also enjoy as a snack.

Ingredients

2 slices whole grain bread
2 tablespoons smooth almond butter
1 small banana
ground cinnamon and nutmeg to taste

Toast the bread and arrange it on an oven-safe plate or a small baking sheet. Spread each slice with 1 tablespoon of almond butter. Slice the banana into rounds of medium thickness and arrange them on top of the almond butter. Sprinkle the surface with cinnamon and nutmeg, then place under the broiler for 2 to 3 minutes, or until the almond butter melts slightly and the bananas begin to brown. Allow to cool and eat with your fingers, or dig in right away with a fork.

DASH-friendly Oatmeal

Oatmeal naturally has properties that make it good for your heart, but many commercial instant products contain large amounts of sugar, sodium and other unhealthy ingredients. If you love a hot, hearty bowl of oats in the morning, this low-cholesterol, salt-free option will satisfy you without cutting back on taste. Fresh fruit and nuts add to the oatmeal's flavor and nutrition profile, making this a breakfast recipe you're sure to love. Try it out on a cold winter morning.

Ingredients

1 ½ cups unsweetened almond milk
1 cup old fashioned rolled oats
¾ cup mixed berries or other chopped fruit
1/8 cup whole pecans
¼ teaspoon vanilla extract
Cinnamon to taste

Combine the almond milk and vanilla in a small sauce pan over medium-high heat. Bring to a gentle simmer and add the oats. Cook, stirring occasionally, for about 5 minutes or until almost all the liquid has been absorbed. Stir in the fruit and serve topped with pecans and cinnamon.

Healthy Homemade Granola

Traditional granolas are full of healthy ingredients such as whole grains, nuts and fruit, but they tend to be heavy on the fat, salt and added sugar. The situation gets worse in the case of some packaged granolas, which add preservatives and other artificial ingredients. This homemade granola recipe is nutritionally dense and concentrates on healthy fats and natural, relatively unrefined sources of sugar. Flax seeds add an extra omega-3 punch, making this recipe a great way to start your day.

Ingredients

3 cups old-fashioned rolled oats
1 cup sliced almonds
1 cup raisins or dried cranberries
4 tablespoons flax seed
¼ cup raw sugar
1/4 cup honey
¼ cup sunflower or canola oil
½ teaspoon vanilla extract
½ teaspoon ground sugar
½ teaspoon allspice
½ teaspoon ground ginger

Combine the oats, almonds, flax, spices and sugar in a large bowl, mixing thoroughly. In a separate bowl combine the honey, oil and vanilla extract. Pour the wet ingredient mixture into the dry ingredients, mixing with a spatula as you pour. Stir until the dry mixture is wet throughout. Lightly grease one to two cookie sheets with sunflower oil or another monounsaturated fat. Pour the wet granola into the pans, patting it into place if necessary. Bake in a 250 degree Fahrenheit oven for 90 minutes or until dry and lightly browned, stirring every 15 minutes. Break up chunks of granola as you stir to create the appropriate consistency. Allow the mixture to cool, then combine with the dried fruit and store in an air-tight container.

Toasted Breakfast Sandwich

Not every DASH-friendly breakfast recipe is sweet. There are also plenty of savory options that combine fresh vegetables with low-sodium, low-cholesterol proteins for a heartier start to your day. If you love eggs for breakfast, this recipe will help you enjoy them without the heart risk associated with large amounts of egg yolk. Flavorful mustard and tomatoes keep the open-faced sandwich interesting, so you won't miss the fat.

Ingredients

2 egg whites
½ cup fresh spinach leaves
1 slice whole grain bread
1 small tomato
1 ½ teaspoons olive oil
1 teaspoon prepared brown mustard
½ ounce slice reduced-fat cheddar cheese
Black pepper and paprika to taste

In a small pan, heat the olive oil to medium-high. Beat the egg whites and add to the hot oil, scrambling them until completely solid. Add the spinach and heat until wilted. Spread the mustard onto the bread and place it on an oven-safe plate or baking sheet. Arrange tomato slices on top of the mustard, then top with the egg mixture and thinly-sliced cheddar cheese. Sprinkle with black pepper and sharp paprika to taste. Bake in an oven or toaster oven at 400 degrees Fahrenheit until the bread is crisp and the cheese is melted and slightly browned.

Main Dishes

Simple Grilled Chicken

This basic chicken dish is easy to make on any outdoor grill. It combines the low cholesterol and white meat of bone-in chicken breasts with flavorful garlic and spices. The finished product is crisp, golden brown and caramelized for an intense flavor. You won't miss the extra fat!

Ingredients

4 bone-in chicken breasts with skin
2 cloves garlic
salt-free herb seasoning mix

Heat a gas or charcoal grill to medium heat. Fold non-stick aluminum foil into a boat shape for each chicken breast. Cut the garlic cloves in half and rub the cut surfaces over the skin of the chicken breasts. Sprinkle with seasoning mix to taste and place the chicken breasts in the boats, skin side down. Grill for 45 minutes or until the center reaches 160 degrees Fahrenheit, turning the chicken once every 10 to 15 minutes.

Basic Barbeque "Pork" Chops

Barbecued pork may sound unhealthy and decadent, but you can substitute other meats to make your favorite pork recipes compatible with the DASH diet. This recipe uses "chops" of boneless chicken thighs, since the dark meat provides similar flavor intensity to that of lean pork. Just make sure you don't overcook it, as the meat can easily dry out with too much heat. Add a fresh salad and this dish is ready to make a complete meal!

1 ½ pounds boneless chicken thighs
10 ounces low sodium condensed tomato soup
3 tablespoons red wine vinegar
2 tablespoons low sodium Worcestershire sauce
1 small onion
¾ cup water
1 teaspoon sharp paprika
1 teaspoon chili powder
¼ teaspoon cinnamon
¼ teaspoon black pepper
1/8 teaspoon cloves

Trim all fat from the chicken, cube, and set aside. Combine all other ingredients in a large bowl, then transfer to a large skillet with high sides. Heat to medium and add the chicken cubes, simmering for 30 minutes or until cooked thoroughly. Serve with bread or 2/3 cup of brown rice.

Miso-Marinated Cod

This spicy Asian fish recipe provides plenty of healthy polyunsaturated omega-3 fatty acids, along with the rich flavors of miso and chili paste. If cod is unavailable, use any firm, flaky white fish that can be cut into thick steaks. Avoid thin species like flounder, which will not cook correctly. While the marinade itself is very salty, the practice of wrapping the fish in a porous material prevents too much salt from getting into the food itself. To make this dish ahead, simply apply the marinade, then freeze the entire dish. Defrost slowly in the refrigerator before cooking normally.

Ingredients

1 pound cod
3 tablespoons low-salt sweet white miso
1 tablespoon garlic-chili paste
2 tablespoons apple juice
2 tablespoons unprocessed cane sugar, such as turbinado

Mix together all raw ingredients except for the fish. Take a piece of plastic wrap and spread it over the counter or a cutting board, then apply a layer of miso marinade a little larger than the total surface area of the fish. Place a piece of cheesecloth on top of the marinade layer. Wrap the cheesecloth around the fish, then apply marinade to the top side. Wrap the plastic around the fish and its wrapping, then place the plastic bundle into a freezer bag. Place in the refrigerator for two hours to overnight.

Remove the fish from the refrigerator and peel away the plastic and cheesecloth layers. Heat a large nonstick frying pan over medium heat and place the fish in it. Cook on both sides until the fish is opaque and flaky throughout. Serve with low-sodium miso soup, rice and Japanese pickles. Discard any unused marinade for safety reasons.

Blackened Beef

Thinly sliced lean top round beef seared with strong spices makes for an exciting and flavorful main dish, especially when you pair it with stewed potatoes, onions and carrots. Finish the dish with tender greens for a recipe that's tasty and nutritious. This blackened beef dish is especially good with crusty low-sodium bread.

Ingredients

1 pound lean top round of beef

6 medium red potatoes

4 large onions

3 large carrots

2 cups low-sodium beef broth

2 cups water

2 cloves garlic

1 bunch kale

2 tablespoons sharp paprika

1 tablespoon dried oregano

1 teaspoon chili powder

1 teaspoon powdered garlic

½ teaspoon black pepper

¼ teaspoon red pepper

¼ teaspoon mustard powder

Place the beef in the freezer until partially frozen. Cut the potatoes into quarters, mince the garlic cloves, slice the carrots into rounds and remove the stems from the kale. Chop the onions very finely to yield about 4 cups. Combine paprika, oregano, garlic powder, chili powder, red and black peppers and dry mustard in a small bowl with a lid. Set aside. Remove beef from freezer and slice it across the grain in strips about 1/8 inch thick. Sprinkle with the seasoning mix, covering all available surfaces. Lightly grease a large heavy skillet or stockpot then preheat over high. Add the meat strips and sear, stirring continuously, for about 5 minutes.

Add the broth and water to the pan to deglaze, then add potatoes and garlic to the skillet. Allow the blackened spices to float to the top. Cover and lower heat to medium, cooking for about 20 minutes or until potatoes are tender. Add the carrots and place the kale on top of the dish. Cover and cook for an additional 10 minutes. This dish can be served right from the skillet or pot.

Feta-ricotta Greek Pizza

Many DASH dieters find that they miss conventional pizza after they start their new healthier way of eating. Getting onto the DASH diet doesn't mean you can't enjoy this classic treat, however. This whole-grain, Greek-inspired recipe provides richness with reduced fat ricotta and feta cheese, plus plenty of tasty vegetables. Adding fennel, mint and olive oil gives this recipe an authentic Mediterranean flavor. Once you learn to make these pizzas at home, you won't miss delivery.

Ingredients

10 ounces fresh or frozen spinach

3 ¼ cups low sodium marinara sauce

1 ¼ cups reduced-fat ricotta cheese

1 ¼ cups fresh mint

1 cup fresh fennel

1 whole grain 14 inch pizza crust or equivalent dough

¾ cup feta cheese crumbles

4 plum tomatoes

1 teaspoon strongly-flavored olive oil

1 teaspoon cornmeal

salt substitute and black pepper to taste

Heat a pizza stone or cookie sheet in the oven at 500

degrees Fahrenheit. Sprinkle a pizza peel with cornmeal to prevent sticking. If you are using a pizza crust, follow package instructions to prepare it for topping.

Chop the mint, tomatoes, fennel and spinach. Heat the olive oil in a large skillet to medium-high. Add the chopped fennel and sauté for five minutes, or until slightly translucent. Reduce the heat to medium-low. Drain all water from the spinach and add it to the fennel. Season with black pepper and salt substitute according to your preferences. Place the raw dough on the pizza peel and transfer it to the baking stone or sheet. Cook for 5 minutes at 500 degrees and remove from oven.

Spread the sauce over the pizza crust, then top with the spinach and fennel mixture. Spoon the ricotta in small quantities over the vegetable mixture, but do not try to spread it. Add feta crumbles and bake for another 15 minutes, or until the crust is cooked completely and the edges are lightly browned. Combine the mint and tomatoes in a separate bowl, then sprinkle them over the surface of the pizza before cutting.

Chinese Restaurant Ginger Beef

American-style Chinese food is rarely compatible with the DASH diet, but many people still miss its exciting flavors. The good news is that you can make your own at home, using far less grease, corn syrup and artificial flavors. You'll retain all the best things about restaurant Chinese dishes and avoid the sometimes sticky sauces and high glycemic index. This dish uses thinly-sliced lean beef, heart-friendly oils and fresh ginger to recreate a classic Chinese restaurant favorite.

Ingredients

¾ pound thinly-sliced flank or sirloin steak

1 medium onion

1 pound mushrooms

1 pound broccoli

2 tablespoons peanut oil

1 tablespoon rice vinegar

1 tablespoon fresh ginger

3 cloves fresh garlic

red pepper flakes to taste

salt substitute to taste

In a deep skillet or wok, heat 1 tablespoon of peanut oil on high. Mince the ginger and onion and add to the hot pan, frying for about a minute. Season with salt substitute to taste. Crush the garlic, slice the mushrooms and chop the broccoli. Add 1 teaspoon of garlic and the mushrooms to the pan. Cook for about 2 minutes, stirring throughout, or until the mushrooms soften and the onions become translucent. Add the broccoli and cook for about 3 minutes or until it is bright green and still slightly crisp. Remove the vegetables to a bowl.

Add the remaining tablespoon of peanut oil to the pan and allow it to heat. Add the beef strips and the remaining garlic, cooking for about 2 minutes. Sprinkle in the vinegar and red pepper flakes, followed by the vegetables. Stir to combine and remove from the heat immediately. Serve over short grain brown rice.

Vegetable Medley Pasta Sauce

The DASH diet works best when you reduce the amount of meat in your diet, but many people don't know where to start. This vegetable-based pasta sauce proves that you don't need to have sausage or beef to make a meal special. It uses readily-available dried herbs and fresh vegetables to provide great flavor without the meat. Serve it with your favorite whole grain pasta.

8 ounces canned low-sodium tomato sauce
6 ounces canned low-sodium tomato paste
2 medium zucchini
2 medium fresh tomatoes
2 small onions
3 cloves garlic
2 tablespoons olive oil
1 tablespoon dried oregano
1 tablespoon dried basil
1 teaspoon dried rosemary
1 cup water

Heat the olive oil in a medium-sized skillet. Mince the garlic and onions. Chop the zucchini and tomatoes coarsely. Add all vegetables to the pan and sauté for about 5 minutes over medium-high heat, or until the onions become slightly translucent. Mix the tomato paste and water in a medium bowl until smooth. Add to the pan, along with the tomato sauce and herbs. Cover and reduce the heat to low. Simmer for 45 minutes or until the sauce reaches the desired consistency. Season with salt substitute if desired.

Portabella Mushroom "Burgers"

Not every sandwich you eat on a bun has to be a hamburger. These grilled or pan-seared Portobello mushrooms are marinated in a tasty mixture of vinegar, garlic, cayenne and olive oil, leaving them anything but bland. When you accompany them with the traditional burger toppings, they make the perfect addition to any picnic, potluck or outdoor grilling occasion. Unlike a conventional hamburger, these sandwiches are low in calories, contain almost no fat, and are cholesterol-free.

Ingredients

4 large portabella mushrooms
5 tablespoons balsamic vinegar
2 tablespoons strongly-flavored olive oil
1 tablespoon raw sugar
1 clove garlic
¼ teaspoon sharp paprika

Wash the mushrooms and remove their stems. Place the mushroom caps in an oven-safe glass dish, stem side up. Mince the garlic and combine it with the olive oil, paprika, sugar and vinegar in a separate small bowl. Drizzle this mixture over the mushrooms. Cover and place in the refrigerator for ½ hour. Flip the mushrooms and marinate for an additional ½ hour.

Preheat the broiler or an outdoor grill to moderate heat. If cooking on a grill, lightly coat the rack with cooking spray. Grill or broil the mushrooms on a rack about 6 inches away from the flame, turning periodically and basting with marinade. Transfer to a plate and allow to rest for a few minutes before serving on whole grain buns with lettuce, tomato, onion and low-sodium pickles.

Sides

Baked Macaroni and Cheese

Macaroni and cheese are classic, hearty and comforting, but traditional recipes rely on butter, cream and very large amounts of full fat cheese. The result may be delightful to the taste buds, but it's hard on your arteries. Consider this version instead, which adds ripe tomatoes and reduced fat dairy to produce a baked dish that's delicious without harming your heart. Eat it as a side to an ordinary dinner or with a salad as a light meal all by itself.

Ingredients

2 cups whole grain macaroni

2 cups skim milk

8 ounces reduced fat cheddar cheese

2 fresh tomatoes

2 tablespoons margarine

1 tablespoon flour

1 small onion

1 teaspoon parsley

¼ teaspoon mustard powder

¼ teaspoon black pepper

Grate the cheese and slice the tomatoes and onion very thinly. Boil the macaroni in water according to package instructions, until al dente. Preheat the oven to 400 degrees Fahrenheit and melt margarine over medium-high heat in a sauce pan. Add mustard, flour, pepper and onion, sautéing until the onion becomes translucent. Stir in the milk slowly and cook until smooth and thickened. Add the cheese and stir until just melted. Drain the macaroni and transfer it to a 2 quart baking dish. Pour the cheese mixture over the macaroni and toss gently. Arrange the tomato slices on top of the dish and sprinkle with parsley. Bake for 20 minutes or until the top browns slightly.

Spicy Steamed Eggplant with Peanut Sauce

While most eggplant dishes are best served warm, this unusual side is an excellent cold option for summer. Preparation is quick and easy, and the finished recipe plates up attractively. Make this Asian-inspired dish on hot summer evenings when you don't feel like cooking. Look for long, thin purple Chinese eggplants and serve with cold noodles or rice.

Ingredients

1 ½ pounds eggplant, preferably Asian varieties
2 tablespoons crunchy peanut butter
1 ½ tablespoons low-sodium soy sauce
1 tablespoon apple juice
½ teaspoon chili paste
1 bunch parsley for garnish

Peel the eggplants using a small knife or vegetable peeler, removing the stem from each one. Wrap each eggplant loosely in damp cheesecloth or paper towels and arrange them in a circle around a microwave-safe plate or vegetable steamer. To prepare in the microwave, cook on the high setting for 5 minutes, turning once halfway through cooking. To prepare on the stovetop, steam in a large pot until the eggplant is soft and slightly translucent. Remove the hot eggplants from the microwave or pan and drop them immediately into a bowl of cold water. Remove the cheesecloth or paper towels and cut the vegetables on the diagonal into slices. Arrange on a plate with parsley and chill in the refrigerator.

For the sauce, combine all other ingredients in a small saucepan. Cook, stirring continuously, over medium-low heat until the peanut butter melts and all ingredients are well combined. Spoon over the chilled eggplant and serve.

Braised Spring Vegetables

This hearty combination of winter and new spring vegetables is a great choice when the weather is just beginning to warm. Serve it alongside your favorite meat as a side dish, or eat it on its own as a light lunch or a snack. This recipe is delicious both hot and cold!

Ingredients

1 pound small red, yellow or purple potatoes
1 large carrot
1 medium onion
1 cup green peas, fresh or frozen
½ pound green beans, fresh or frozen
1 clove garlic
½ tablespoon low-sodium soy sauce
1 teaspoon olive oil

Wash all the vegetables and cut the potatoes, carrot and onion into bite size pieces. Top, tail and snap the green beans if you are using fresh vegetables. Mince the garlic. Heat the olive oil in the bottom of a heavy skillet or pan over medium-low heat. Add the potatoes and cook for about 10 minutes or until they begin to brown, stirring occasionally. Add the carrots and cook for another 10 minutes, until both vegetables have begun to tenderize.

Add the sliced onions and garlic. Cook until they become transparent. Fill the pan with water to cover the potatoes and add the green vegetables. Cook until the beans and peas are bright green and tender, but not mushy. Season with soy sauce at the very end of the cooking process.

Rice Pilaf with Saffron

This rice dish is inspired by South Asian pilau, which often include fruit and nuts. Any brown rice will provide the nutty flavor and fiber that are ideal in this recipe, but the best choice is a very dark brown, strong-tasting rice that will provide an appealing contrast for the apricots. Serve this dish hot, as a side for curries or kebabs. If saffron is not available, you can substitute safflower or turmeric for a slightly different flavor.

2 ¼ cups vegetable stock
1 ¼ cups long grain brown rice
¼ cup pistachios
¼ cup dried apricots
3 tablespoons orange juice
1 ½ tablespoons canola, coconut or sunflower oil
¼ teaspoon saffron
salt substitute to taste

Combine the rice, stock and saffron in a medium saucepan. Bring to a boil over high heat. Reduce the heat to low and cover, simmering until the rice has become tender and absorbed all the liquid. Transfer to a large bowl. Combine the orange juice, oil and salt substitute in a small bowl. Pour this mixture over the rice. Chop the apricots. Heat a small skillet to medium and add the fruit and nuts, stirring continuously until the pistachios brown slightly and develop an oily appearance. Toss the fruit and nuts with the flavored rice to mix. Serve right away.

Spicy Garlic Green Beans

Green beans are a classic side dish for all kinds of cuisines, but too many people boil out the nutrients or serve them with copious amounts of butter. Instead of weighing down your beans, celebrate their crisp flavor with this spicy but appealing recipe. Blanching helps set the color and ensures an attractive dish, while a quick sauté with strongly-flavored
ingredients keeps the beans from blending into the background.

Ingredients

1 pound fresh, raw green beans
1 sweet red bell pepper
2 cloves garlic
2 teaspoons extra virgin olive oil
1 teaspoon dark sesame oil
½ teaspoon salt substitute
½ teaspoon chili paste
¼ teaspoon black pepper

Top and tail the beans, removing any strings, and snap them into 2 inch pieces. Bring a large pan of water to a boil over high heat and add the snapped beans. Cook for about 3 minutes, until they become bright green and crisp-tender. Remove the beans from the water and plunge them immediately into a bowl of ice water. Drain and place in a large bowl.

Remove the stem, ribs and seeds from the red bell pepper and cut it into thin strips about 2 inches in length. Heat the olive oil in a large frying pan over medium heat. Add the pepper, stir-frying for about a minute. Add the beans and cook for and additional minute. Crush the garlic and combine with the chili paste, salts substitute and pepper in a small bowl. Add this mixture to the vegetables, stirring to coat. Serve drizzled with sesame oil.

Salads

Spicy Tuna Salad

While the DASH diet emphasizes healthy foods that are lower in fat and cholesterol, that doesn't mean you can't enjoy your favorites. This tuna salad recipe relies on flavorful tomatoes, onions, limes and jalapenos, allowing you to reduce the sodium and cholesterol in other ingredients without losing out on taste.

Ingredients

12 oz. low sodium tuna (about 2 cans)
1/8 cup olive oil or low-fat mayonnaise
1 jalapeno pepper
1 tomato
1 small sweet onion
1 small lime

Drain the water from the tuna and place it in a medium bowl with the mayonnaise. Remove the stem, seeds and ribs from the pepper, dicing it finely. Dice the tomato and the onion. Add the vegetables and lime juice to the bowl and mix thoroughly. Serve with DASH-friendly crackers or bread.

Tabbouleh with Tomatoes

Tabbouleh is a mint-flavored cold salad popular in northern Africa and Western Asia. When made with whole grains, it provides plenty of nutritious fiber, along with refreshing vegetables. The tart flavor of this salad can take a little time to get used to, but it's an extremely welcome change when hot weather comes along. Serve tabbouleh on its own or as a side with kebabs or barbecued meats and vegetables.

Ingredients

½ pound whole grain bulgur wheat
½ pound cucumbers
½ pound fresh tomatoes
3 medium red onions
2 cups flat leaf parsley
½ cup fresh mint
3 lemons
1 tablespoon olive oil
½ teaspoon black pepper

Place the wheat in a large bowl and cover it with water. Soak for one hour or longer, until the grain has absorbed water and plumped. Chop all the vegetables into small cubes or dice and set aside. Drain the bulgur and mix it with the vegetables. Juice the lemons, removing the seeds but reserving the pulp. Add the lemon juice, herbs, oil and pepper to the mixture. Place it in a covered bowl and refrigerate for one to 12 hours. This salad can be stored as is for several days or up to a week with the onions omitted.

Edamame Salad

Fresh, steamed soybeans are known as Edamame in Japan, and are eaten as an appetizer or part of other dishes. When served cold, these beans also make a great salad ingredient. This recipe combines them with cherry tomatoes, fresh mint, dill and scallions. A light oil and vinegar dressing finishes it for a fresh-tasting start to any meal. Try it with a little feta or other salty cheese for added contrast.

Ingredients

½ pound fresh Edamame

1 pint cherry or grape tomatoes

¼ cup red wine vinegar

1 ½ tablespoons extra virgin olive oil

1 scallion

1 small bunch fresh dill weed

1 small bunch fresh mint

¼ teaspoon black pepper

Place the soybeans in a steamer over about an inch of water. Cover and steam for approximately 5 minutes, or until the pods are bright green and the beans are crisp-tender. Rinse with cold water and remove from the pods. Set the beans aside in a medium bowl and refrigerate. Chop the mint and dill finely. Slice the green onion. Cut large cherry tomatoes into halves, leaving small ones whole. Combine tomatoes, green onion, mint and dill in a medium bowl. Mix oil, vinegar and black pepper in a small bowl and pour over the salad. Serve chilled.

Raw Okra Salad

Many people associate okra with slimy boiled preparations or greasy fried food. This unusual member of the mallow family doesn't have to be cooked, however. When sliced carefully and served raw, it has an exciting crispness and lacks any unappealing mucilage. Combine it with spicy mixed salad greens, jicama and sweet peppers for a refreshing salad that's a little outside the usual fare.

Ingredients

1 cup fresh okra
1/3 pound fresh salad greens
1 pound jicama
1 small sweet red bell pepper
4 tablespoons low sodium poppy-seed salad dressing
¼ teaspoon salt substitute
1/4 teaspoon black pepper

Remove the stems from the okra and slice them in half vertically, using a clean, absolutely dry knife. Wipe the knife off between pieces to reduce mucilage production. Remove the stem, seeds and ribs from the pepper and cut it into strips. Peel and slice the jicama into matchsticks. Combine the okra, salad greens, pepper and jicama in a large bowl. Toss gently and season with salt substitute and fresh pepper. Top with poppy-seed dressing and serve immediately.

Tomato-Zucchini Salad with Eggs

Squash and tomatoes are abundant and at their best in the heat of summer, which is the best time to make this refreshing salad. The addition of eggs provides a little more heartiness and allows this dish to act as a light lunch or a starter. For a slightly different flavor, consider using different types of fresh herbs.

Ingredients

2 pounds zucchini
2 pounds ripe tomatoes
6 to 8 eggs
½ cup fresh basil
Dressing:
2 tablespoons extra virgin olive oil
¼ cup red wine vinegar
1 tablespoon fresh parsley
1 teaspoon raw sugar

Combine all dressing ingredients in a glass bowl and mix thoroughly. Set aside. Slice the zucchini and tomatoes into thin rounds. Bring one large and one small pot of water to a boil. Place the eggs in one pot, immediately cover, and reduce heat. Plunge the zucchini rounds into the larger pot for 2 to 3 minutes. Remove from the pot and place immediately in ice water. Drain completely and arrange alternately with the tomato slices on a large plate. Drain the eggs and place them in a bowl of ice water. Peel and slice, arranging the slices on top of the zucchini and tomato rounds. Cover with basil leaves, then drizzle vinegar mixture over the entire platter.

Low Cholesterol Potato Salad

Traditional potato salad is a must at many picnics, but it's loaded with cholesterol, fat and sodium. All of these ingredients can be hazardous for your heart, so many DASH dieters feel as though potato salad is off the menu. This recipe offers much of the same creamy taste and texture, but without the fat and salt. Bring it to your next picnic and no one will ever worry about it being "health food."

Ingredients

1 pound yellow or red waxy potatoes

1 large yellow sweet onion

2 stalks celery

1 large carrot

¼ cup reduced-calorie mayonnaise

2 tablespoons dill weed

2 tablespoons red wine vinegar

1 tablespoon prepared brown mustard

Boil the potatoes in their skins, allow to cool, and dice. Mince the onion and dill weed. Dice the carrot and celery into small pieces. Combine the mayonnaise, mustard, vinegar, pepper and dill in a large bowl. Stir in the vegetables, mixing to coat the pieces completely.

Cover and refrigerate for one hour to overnight to allow the flavors to mingle. Serve chilled.

Soups

Nutrient-packed Kale Soup

The unique, slightly-nutty taste of kale makes this soup an interesting and satisfying starter for any cold season meal, while providing a wide range of healthy vitamins. Adding homemade croutons gives this creamy recipe a hearty crunch without too much fat or too many processed carbohydrates. Plus, their freshness will help them outshine any store-bought option. Enjoy this soup whenever the weather turns chilly and kale is readily available.

Ingredients

6 cups fresh kale leaves
4 cups low sodium broth or stock, preferably vegetable
3 medium red potatoes
1 small white onion
1 tablespoon olive oil
1 tablespoon fresh thyme
1 clove fresh garlic
½ teaspoon black pepper
¼ teaspoon salt substitute
Croutons:

2 cups day old whole grain bread pieces
2 tablespoons olive oil
1 tablespoon fresh thyme
1 tablespoon fresh parsley
1 teaspoon garlic powder

Trim the kale leaves and remove any tough ribs. Chop the onion and the potatoes into small dice. Crush the garlic. Heat 1 tablespoon of olive oil in a heavy pan over medium heat and sauté the chopped onion, crushed garlic and fresh thyme for 7 to 8 minutes or until the onions are transparent. Add the diced potatoes, salt substitute and pepper. Stir well and cook for another 10 minutes or until the potatoes have begun to soften. Remove the cover and add the kale. Cook uncovered for 5 minutes, then add broth, cover and heat for an additional 5 minutes or until the kale becomes bright green and tender. Place half of the soup in a food processor or blender and process until completely smooth. Return this mixture to the saucepan and mix thoroughly.

Croutons: Cut or break bread into pieces approximately ½ inch across. Combine garlic powder, 2 tablespoons olive oil and herbs in a large bowl and add the bread. Toss to coat the outside of the bread but do not allow the oil to soak in. Place croutons on a baking sheet lined with foil and bake at 350 degrees for about 10 minutes or until the outsides are crisp and golden. Cool and use to top bowls of hot soup.

Meatless Lentil Chili

This tasty vegetarian alternative to conventional chili is hearty and flavorful, with bulgur wheat and lentils replacing the usual fatty beef and chili beans. If you're trying to reduce the number of days on which you eat meat, this chili is a great way to start. Serve with diced scallions, low fat sour cream or a DASH-friendly cornbread. For a more interesting chili, substitute red, yellow or black lentils for the traditional brown variety.

Ingredients

3 cups low-sodium vegetable broth
2 cups or one can chopped tomatoes
1 cup bulgur wheat
1 cup dried lentils
1 medium white onion
4 cloves garlic
2 tablespoons canola oil
2 ½ tablespoons chili powder
1 tablespoon cumin powder
½ teaspoon cinnamon
Salt substitute and pepper to taste

Heat the oil to medium-high in a large pot. Mince the onion and garlic, then add them to the pot and cook for

5 minutes, stirring continuously. When the alliums have become slightly translucent, add the wheat and lentils, followed by the broth. Stir to combine, then add the tomatoes and spices. Bring to a boil over high heat, then reduce to low and cover. Simmer for 30 minutes or until the lentils just begin to fall apart. Add salt substitute and pepper to taste and serve hot.

Tangy Carrot Curry

This smooth soup contains plenty of exciting spices, along with protein-rich low fat yogurt and bright, tangy cilantro. The result is an antioxidant-filled dish you'll enjoy with a fresh salad and a slice of homestyle whole-grain bread. For a spicier version, substitute cayenne or Thai peppers for the jalapeno.

Ingredients

5 cups low-sodium vegetable stock
1 pound carrots
1 large yellow onion
1 jalapeno pepper
¼ cup cilantro leaves
¼ cup low fat unsweetened yogurt
2 tablespoons lime or lemon juice
1 tablespoon sunflower oil
1 tablespoon fresh ginger
2 cloves garlic
2 teaspoons Madras curry powder
1 teaspoon black mustard seeds
salt substitute to taste

Heat the olive oil in a large saucepan to medium. Mince the garlic and ginger and chop the onion finely. Add the mustard seed to the oil and allow it to pop, then add the ginger, garlic and onion. Cook for about 5 minutes, stirring continuously, or until the onions become translucent but not brown. Remove the stem, seeds and ribs of the jalapeno and chop it finely, then add to the pan along with the curry powder. Chop the carrots roughly and sauté with the other ingredients for about 3 minutes, or until the seasonings begin to toast. Pour in about half of the stock and bring the whole pot to a boil over high heat. Reduce to medium-low and simmer for about 5 minutes, or until the carrots become tender.

Remove the soup from the pot and place it in a blender or food processor. Process until the liquid is smooth, in batches if necessary, and return to the pan. Stir in the remaining stock and reheat. Add yogurt, cilantro and lime juice, as well as salt substitute to taste. Garnish with additional cilantro and limes before serving.

Cream of Wild Rice Soup with Fennel

Traditional cream of rice soups are extremely comforting, but they're also heavy on butter, cream and refined carbohydrates, making them unsuitable for the DASH diet. Instead, consider this version. It gets its creaminess from white beans and low fat milk and includes vitamin-packed kale and carrots. If wild rice is unavailable in your area, consider substituting any long grain brown rice, such as Basmati, or red rice.

2 cups 1 percent or skim milk
2 cups low-sodium vegetable stock
1 ½ cups kale
1 cup cooked white beans, unsalted
¼ cup wild rice
2 stalks celery
1 large sweet onion
1 large carrot
1 tablespoon fresh parsley
½ tablespoon vegetable oil
1 teaspoon fennel
1 teaspoon black pepper
salt substitute to taste

Place wild rice in a small pot and cover with water. Bring to a boil over high heat, then reduce heat and simmer until the rice has become tender but chewy, or about one hour. Dice the carrot, celery, onion and parsley. Heat the vegetable oil in a large pot over medium heat, then add the onion, carrot, celery and spices. Cook, stirring periodically, until the onions are translucent, the carrots have become slightly tender. Add the parsley, kale and stock. Season with salt substitute to taste.

Combine the milk with the cooked white beans in a blender or food processor. Puree until smooth and add gradually to the soup, stirring continuously. Bring to a simmer and add the cooked rice. Simmer for an additional 30 minutes or until flavors have diffused. Serve with crusty low-sodium bread.

Hearty Turkey Soup

This recipe isn't just a way to use up the leftovers from a big holiday meal, it's also a hearty low-sodium option that includes plenty of healthy winter vegetables. Serve big bowls of this dish with rice or bread as meals on their own, or as a side for lunch or dinner.

Ingredients

Carcass from one turkey
2 quarts low-sodium chicken or vegetable broth
1 quart water
4 large yellow onions
1 large turnip
1 pound carrots
2 cups tomatoes, fresh or canned
2 cups cooked white beans, home-cooked or canned
½ pound light turkey
¼ cup hulled whole barley
1/3 cup fresh parsley
½ teaspoon black pepper
¼ teaspoon thyme
1 bay leaf
salt substitute to taste

Place the turkey carcass in a large stockpot with the

broth and water. Bring to a boil over high heat. Chop one onion into quarters and add to the pot. Reduce the heat, cover, and allow the pot to simmer for an hour. Remove all solids from the pot and place the stock in the refrigerator for 2 hours to overnight. Skim off any fat from the cooled broth and discard. Return the broth to its original pot.

Chop the carrots, turnip, tomatoes and remaining onions and add them to the broth. Add the bay leaf, beans, barley, herbs and spices to the mixture, stirring to combine. Cut the turkey meat into bite-sized chunks and add to the pot. Bring the entire mixture to a simmer, then cover and allow to cook for an hour or until all the vegetables have softened. Serve immediately.

DASH Diet 5-Day Sample Menu

Deciding how to eat on the DASH diet plan can be tricky if you're not used to dealing with its rules. Here's a quick 5-day sample menu using some recipes from this book to help you get started. There's no reason to stick to just this menu, however. You can mix and match the recipes or use foods of your own. Just make sure that you stick to the guidelines set forth earlier in this book and it'll be hard to go wrong!

Day 1

Breakfast: Fresh orange juice, whole grain toast with low-sugar fruit spread, DASH-Friendly Oatmeal

Lunch: Tangy Carrot Curry, fresh vegetable crudités, brown rice
Snack: almonds, hazelnuts or cashews, fresh peach or nectarine

Dinner: Blackened Beef, Tabbouleh with Tomatoes, Chewy Fruit Bars

Day 2

Breakfast: Healthy Homemade Granola, fresh strawberries, skim milk

Lunch: Miso-Marinated Cod, Edamame Salad, hot green tea

Snack: fat-free, low-sugar yogurt, graham crackers

Dinner: Chinese Restaurant Ginger Beef, brown rice, fresh oranges

Day 3

Breakfast: Toasted Breakfast Sandwich, fresh orange juice

Lunch: Spicy Tuna Salad on whole grain bread with lettuce and tomato,
Sugar Free Agua Fresca

Snack: Pretzels, raisins, sunflower seeds

Dinner: Feta-ricotta Greek Pizza, lettuce hearts, olives

Day 4

Breakfast: Peanut Butter and Banana Smoothie, whole grain bagel with light cream cheese

Lunch: Meatless lentil chili, low-sodium cornbread, tomatoes, low-fat sour cream

Snack: Vegetable Sushi

Dinner: Simple Grilled Chicken, Braised Spring Vegetables, vanilla wafers

Day 5

Breakfast: Chewy Fruit Bars, Spicy, Sweet and Tangy Herbal Tea

Lunch: Tomato-Zucchini Salad with Eggs, whole grain pasta with
Vegetable Medley Pasta Sauce

Snack: apple, whole grain crackers

Dinner: Portabella Mushroom "Burgers", Low Cholesterol Potato Salad, low fat frozen yogurt

Modifying the 5-Day Meal Plan

Because every person has different calorie requirements, it's hard to say how much you'll need to eat of these foods at any given meal. If you take a little time to look at your activity level and personal habits, you'll have an easier time choosing the right calorie level for you. The main DASH diet offers 1,200, 1,600, 2,000 and 2,400 calorie options for various amounts of activity and various metabolisms. In general, if you're hoping to lose weight, consider choosing a calorie goal that's one rung lower than the one you need to maintain.

That means that if you're relatively active but overweight, you could move down from the 2,000 calories that you probably need to stay at your current weight, choosing a 1,600 calorie per day diet, instead. You'd aim to get the same 4 to 5 servings of fruits and vegetables per day, as well as the same 3 to 4 servings of low fat dairy, nuts and beans, but you'd limit your meat consumption to just 5 ounces per day and cut back on fats and sweets. It may take a little while to figure things out, but you can help it along by doubling up on low calorie vegetables, fruits and non-fat dairy while limiting meat, cheese and grain consumption.

Conclusion

The average American diet is high in unhealthy fried food and high-fat meat and dairy sources, as well as too much sugar. The result, for many people, is skyrocketing blood pressure and an increased risk of heart disease and stroke. If you're worried that your health could be at risk, it's time to take steps.

That means moving to the DASH diet and avoiding unhealthy foods in favor of rich, flavorful options that are low in fat and high in vitamins. While it's true that the adjustment period may take a little longer than you expect, all these recipes will help you make the transition. You won't miss the fat or extra sugar! Just focus on the healthy foods that you can eat and work to make fruits and vegetables a regular part of your routine. Your heart and your waistline will thank you.

Section 2: Grain Free Recipes

There's something absolutely delicious about a freshly baked loaf of bread, a crispy waffle, or a tasty cake hot out of the oven! These foods all have one thing in common: they're made with grain or wheat flour. Cooking with wheat flour and grain is something that everyone does, and it produces a whole lot of delicious foods.

Unfortunately for many, grain and wheat are things that they cannot enjoy. Gluten intolerance can be a serious problem for many people, and they are unable to eat foods that contain lots of grain or wheat. When they do, they have serious digestive problems, or their body can react strongly and negatively to the gluten in the grain that they are eating.

Gluten has been linked to a number of problems. Interestingly enough, the body often sees gluten as being a foreign substance that it can't process. While gluten is commonly found in the food we eat, it wasn't always part of our diet. The human body can't always process this gooey, sticky protein easily, and it can be a bit hard on the body if you happen to be sensitive to it. Even those without celiac problems may not be able to handle the gluten, as their bodies react to the "foreign substance" by attacking it with antibodies.

Cutting grain out of your diet can help to reduce your risk of health problems, especially if you have celiac disorder or other gluten-sensitive problems. However, even for those that don't have these health problems, it may be a good idea to cut gluten out of your diet. Many people don't have celiac disease, and yet they still experience the drawbacks of eating gluten.

In an article in the New Zealand edition of Stuff magazine, an article by a world-renowned expert on food allergies, Dr. Rodney Ford, states, "Gluten causes tiredness, anxiety and stress. The medical world accepts it can damage the gut, but it can also damage the brain, skin and nerves. Until now, many of these illnesses have been blamed on everything from stress at home to other medical conditions, including depression." [1]

Cutting gluten out of your life isn't just something you can do to prevent celiac problems, but it can be good for your health. Many holistic doctors and therapists will recommend cutting it from your diet, as it carries the risk of causing negative side effects.

Did you know that eliminating grain and gluten can be beneficial to your body? The benefits include:

- Reduced risk of IBS or other digestive problems
- Less chance of becoming fatigued, depressed, nauseous, or developing stomach cramps
- Boost in your energy levels
- Reduced body fat percentage
- Increase in lean muscle tissue
- Lowered blood pressure
- Improved mood and sense of wellbeing
- As you can see, there are many great reasons to cut grain from your diet!

"But," you may say, "all of my favorite foods are made with grain! How can I cut grain out of my diet and still enjoy the food I'm eating?"

Don't worry about it! In this book, you'll find plenty of delicious recipes that you can make without needing to use grain, and you can whip up your favorite dishes and still make them gluten-free. You'll have to spend a bit of money to stock your house with some ingredients you probably don't have right now, but you'll be amazed at how many delicious foods you can make without using grain.

Enjoy the book, and happy grain-free cooking!

Tasty Grain Free Recipes

Grain Free Breaded Chicken

There's nothing like some breaded chicken to kick off your lunch in style, but bread crumbs have wheat, right? Here is a quick and easy recipe you can use to make breaded chicken without the bread...

Ingredients

For this dish, you will need:

1 large chicken breast
1 cup of almond flour
½ cup of Kraft's Parmesan Cheese
Thyme
Basil
Oregano
½ cup of butter
Red or crushed chili pepper
Garlic powder
Salt and pepper, to taste

Preparation:

To begin, slice the chicken breast into steaks -- preferably about three steaks from each half of the breast. You should have about 6 medium steaks from the breast.

Preheat your oven to about 350 F. Use a bit of butter to grease the bottom of a baking tray.

In a bowl, combine the almond flour with the Parmesan cheese. Sprinkle in about a teaspoon each of basil, thyme, and oregano, and add in a pinch of crushed red pepper for some spice. A teaspoon of garlic powder will help to add the flavor you want, and a bit of salt and black pepper will round out the flavors.

In a saucepan, melt the butter. Dip the chicken steaks into the butter, ensuring that the entire surface of the chicken is coated well. Roll the buttered strips in the almond flour, and make sure that they are properly coated with the flour mixture.

Place the steaks onto your baking tray, laying them as flat as possible. Transfer the tray into the oven, and let the steaks cook for about 20 minutes. They should be a wonderful golden brown, and they will be absolutely delightful to eat! (Check to make sure that they aren't pink in the center, as that's a sign that the chicken is undercooked.)

Sesame Seed Chicken Fried Steak

Want to eat that Southern-style chicken fried steak that your mama used to make you? This simple recipe won't make it exactly like the regular steak, but it's as close as you'll get while on a gluten-free diet!

Ingredients

For this dish, you will need:
4 large steaks, sliced fairly thin
2 eggs
½ cup of almond flour
1/3 cup of sesame seeds
1/4 cup of flax seeds
Chicken bouillon powder
Basil
Bay leaves
Garlic powder
Salt and black pepper, to taste

Preparation:

To begin, place a pan on the stove to heat, and add in enough oil to deep fry your breaded steak. Let the oil heat as you go about preparing the rest of the meal.

Crack the 2 eggs into a bowl, and beat them vigorously to combine the egg and yolk. Add a pinch of salt into the eggs.

Combine the almond flour, a pinch each of chicken bouillon, garlic powder, salt, and pepper, and the flax seeds in a bowl. Add the sesame seeds into the bowl, and crush three bay leaves in your hands to add them into the mix. Use a fork to stir the dry ingredients together, and make sure that they're properly combined before moving on.

Dip each steak into the eggs, and roll the dipped meat into the flour and seed mixture. Make sure that the entire surface of the meat has been properly coated. If you want to really get the flour coating on right, you can roll the meat in the flour before dipping it into the egg, and roll it a second time after dipping to ensure that the layer of flour is very thick.

Place the steaks in the hot oil one at a time, and cook them until they are golden brown. Remove them from the pan once they are properly cooked, and place them on a plate with paper towels beneath and above them to soak up the oil.

Let the steaks sit until they are all cooked, transfer onto

a plate, and serve.

Gluten and Sugar-Free Gingerbread Cake

Want a delicious dessert to make your Christmas celebrations complete? This gluten and sugar-free gingerbread cake will have all of the flavor of the holiday, but with none of the unhealthy nutrients that you're trying to avoid!

Ingredients:

For this cake, you will need:
½ cup of coconut flour
1 cup of amaranth flour
1 cup of buckwheat flour
2 tablespoons of flax meal (For those who want the non-vegan version of this cake, use 2 eggs instead of the flax meal. It will make the cake a bit fluffier, and will help to round out the flavors nicely.)
2 ½ teaspoons of baking soda
Ground cinnamon
Ground ginger
Ground cloves
Ground nutmeg
Salt
Water
¾ cup of agave nectar
¾ cup of molasses

Canola oil

Fresh ginger

Lemon zest

Preparation:

To begin, turn on the oven and let it heat to 350 F. As the oven is heating, prepare the cake.

Combine the coconut flour, amaranth flour, buckwheat flour, and baking soda in a bowl. Add in 2 teaspoons of cinnamon, the same amount of ground ginger, half a teaspoon each of cloves, salt, and nutmeg, and a teaspoon or two of lemon zest. Stir the ingredients well to combine.

In a separate bowl, combine the flax meal with a few tablespoons of water, and stir in the agave, the molasses, ¾ of a cup of canola oil, and a couple of teaspoons of the grated fresh ginger. Mix these ingredients together well, and pour them into the bowl with the dry ingredients. Stir the wet and dry ingredients together to make the batter for the cake, and add about a cup of boiling water to your final batter.

Once the water has been properly mixed in with the rest of the ingredients, pour the cake batter into a buttered baking pan. Place the pan into the oven, and let it cook for about 40 minutes.

You'll find that a toothpick or knife inserted into the center of the cake will come out clean, and it will let you know that your cake is ready to enjoy.

Cut once the cake has cooled a bit, and serve.

Gluten Free Waffles

There's nothing like a heaping stack of waffles to get your morning started the right way, but your regular waffles are loaded with grain and gluten. These delicious grain-free waffles will be the perfect breakfast, and it will help you to enjoy what you're eating without having to worry about adding grain to your diet.

Ingredients

For this dish, you will need:
1 cup of rice flour
1/3 cups of potato starch (not all cornstarch products are gluten-free)
3 tablespoons of tapioca flour
1 ½ teaspoons of baking powder
½ teaspoon of baking soda
Salt
Xanthan gum
Buttermilk
Sugar substitute
2 eggs
Canola oil
2 cups of water

Preparation:

To begin, heat your waffle iron. It takes about 5 to 10 minutes for the waffle iron to heat -- depending on the brand -- so make sure that it's heating as you go about preparing the waffles.

Mix the rice flour, potato starch, tapioca flour, baking soda, and baking powder together in a bowl. Add in about half a teaspoon of salt, and the same amount of xanthan gum. Mix the dry ingredients together, and be sure that they are properly combined before moving on to the next step.

Crack the two eggs into another bowl, and add in the water. Add about 3 tablespoons of the oil, and mix the ingredients together well. Stir them in with the dry ingredients, and mix until you get the waffle batter you want. The batter will be a bit thick, so add buttermilk to produce the desired consistency for the waffle batter. Make sure that there are no lumps.

Use some spray cooking oil to grease the waffle iron, or use regular oil on a paper towel to cover the iron with a thin layer of oil. Pour the batter into the heated iron, and close the lid. Watch the waffle iron until the light turns off, and use a fork to remove the cooked waffle from the waffle maker.

Serve while hot, and enjoy the delicious, crunchy waffles!

Buckwheat Pancakes

For those of you who just can't stay away from those flapjacks, this pancake recipe will be the perfect grain-free solution for you! You'll still be able to have a tall stack of delicious pancakes, but without worrying about gluten or grain.

Ingredients

For this dish, you will need:
1 ½ cups of buckwheat flour
3 tablespoons of sugar (use sugar alternative for a low-sugar meal)
Salt
1 teaspoon of baking soda
Unsalted butter
1 egg
Buttermilk

Preparation:

To begin, place a frying pan on the stove to heat. Make sure that it has been properly heated before placing the batter onto the pan, so give it time to warm up as you make the pancakes.

Mix the flour, sugar, and baking soda together in a bowl.
Add in about a teaspoon of salt. Stir the ingredients well
to combine.

Crack your egg in another bowl, and beat to combine
the yolk and white.

Melt the butter in a saucepan or the microwave, and
pour the melted butter over the flour mixture -- stirring
as you pour. Add the egg into the mix, and pour in about
a cup of buttermilk as well. Stir the batter together, and
you'll have a fairly thick mixture. Keep pouring in
buttermilk until your pancakes have reached the desired
consistency, and stir to ensure that there are no lumps.

Once the batter has been prepared, pour it into a
pitcher or an empty ketchup bottle. Gently pour or
squeeze the batter onto your heated pan, which you will
have coated with a bit of oil to butter to prevent the
pancakes from sticking.

Cook until the top of the pancake is riddled with
bubbles, and flip it over to cook on the other side for
about 20 seconds.

Once the batter has been used up, you'll have a delicious
stack of healthy buckwheat pancakes that are grain-free

and fairly low calorie!

Grain-Free Cornbread

You can't have chili beans without some delicious cornbread, and there are so many other dishes that won't be complete without this delicious savory baked bread. Don't worry about it being high in grain, as we've substituted the ingredients in the bread for grain-free ones!

Ingredients

For this dish, you will need:
1 ½ cups of cornmeal
1 cup of millet flour
1 cup of rice flour
2 eggs
Water
Vegetable oil
¼ cup of sugar
1 tablespoon of baking powder
Salt

Preparation:

To begin, heat your oven to about 400 degrees. This way, it will be hot enough to cook the bread, but it won't be so hot that the bread will burn.

Use a bit of butter to grease a 9x9 baking dish, and set it aside as you prepare the bread.

In a bowl, crack and beat the eggs vigorously to combine the yolk and egg white. Heat 1 ½ cups of water until they are lukewarm, and add them into the eggs. Drop in ¼ cup of canola or vegetable oil, and mix the ingredients well until they are properly blended.

In a separate bowl, mix the millet flour, rice flour, and cornmeal together. Add in the white sugar, the baking powder, and about a teaspoon of salt. Make sure that the dry ingredients are all mixed together properly, and hollow out a hole in the center of the bowl.

Pour the wet ingredients into the hollowed center of the flour mixture, and use a whisk to stir the ingredients together properly. Whisk and stir until you are sure that there are no lumps, which could take a few minutes.

Once you're sure there are no lumps, pour the batter into the greased baking pan. Place the pan into the oven, and let it cook for about 20 minutes. You can tell that it's cooked by pressing on the surface of the bread. If it's properly done, the corn bread will spring back up when you press gently on it.

Remove from the oven, let the cornbread cool for a few minutes, and serve while still warm.

Curried Quinoa

This delicious side dish is made without any grain, which means that you can eat it whenever you want! The quinoa is a much lower-calorie alternative to rice, but it will be a delicious alternative that will make the dish absolutely fantastic!

Ingredients:

For this dish, you will need:
1 cup of quinoa
Olive oil
1 onion
Garlic
2 cups of chicken broth
Curry powder
Ancho chili powder
Salt and pepper

Preparation:

To begin, place a skillet on the stove to heat. Bring it to medium heat, and pour a couple of tablespoons of olive oil into the pan.

Chop the onion very finely, and add between 3 and 5

cloves of garlic -- depending on your flavor preference. Cook the aromatics in the oil, leaving them in the pan for about 5 minutes to ensure that you have extracted the flavor from them. Add the quinoa into the pan, and cook the seed in the oil until it is lightly toasted.

Once you're done cooking the quinoa, pour the chicken broth into the pan. Cover the pan, and let the broth heat until it begins to boil. Stir in about a tablespoon each of the curry powder and Mexican chili powder, and cover the pan once again.

Turn the heat down to let the quinoa simmer, and let it cook on low heat for about 25 minutes. The quinoa should be soft and tasty, and you can add a bit of salt and pepper to add the flavor you want for the dish. (Serve as the starch with nearly any protein, and it will be a delicious companion for your meal!)

Roasted Almond Cookies

Want to enjoy a delicious dessert without getting into the grain-loaded cookie jar? These cookies are quick and easy to make, and you'll find that they're the perfect grain-free solution to help you stay true to your gluten-free diet!

Ingredients:

For this dish, you will need:
1 cup of raw almonds
½ cup of maple syrup
1 cup of oat flour
Almond extract

Preparation:

Preheat the oven to about 275 F, which will be hot enough to toast the almonds.

Place the cup of almonds onto a baking sheet, and put them in the oven. Let them heat until they become golden brown and are releasing a delightful scent, which will take about 40 minutes. Be careful that they don't burn.

Once the almonds are cooked, remove them from the oven and set them aside to cool. After they have cooled down enough, run them through your food processor to produce a fine almond flour.

Mix the flour in a bowl together with the oat flour, maple syrup, and almond extract.

Turn the heat of the oven up to 350 F, and let it heat.

As the oven is heating, use your hands to form the dough into 6 balls. Press the balls gently to flatten them a bit, until they are about half an inch thick. Place the cookies onto a greased baking sheet, and put the sheet in the oven.

Let the cookies bake for about 12 minutes, but keep a close eye on them because the edges can burn very quickly. They will become browned and crisp around the edges of the cookie, and that's how you'll know that they're done.

Remove them from the oven, let them cool, and enjoy!

Grain-Free Zucchini Bread

Most people think of banana bread or carrot cake as being the only vegetable-laden desserts that you can make, but you'll find that zucchini bread will be a delicious alternative that will be just as healthy and tasty! Thanks to the grain-free recipe, you won't have to worry about the gluten.

Ingredients:

For this dish, you will need:
1 cup of teff flour
1 cup of buckwheat flour
Baking soda
Salt
Baking powder
3 eggs
Lemon zest
Cinnamon
1 cup of apple sauce
½ cup of maple syrup
Coconut oil
Vanilla extract
2 cups of grated zucchini
1 cup of raisins and almonds mixed

Preparation:

To begin, turn on your oven and pre-heat it to about 350 degrees. As it's heating, move on to the next step.

Mix the buckwheat and teff flours together in a bowl, and add in a tablespoon of cinnamon, a teaspoon of salt and lemon zest each, 2 teaspoons of the baking soda, and ¼ teaspoon of baking powder. Stir well to ensure that the ingredients are properly combined before moving on.

In a separate bowl, combine the apple sauce and maple syrup together, and crack the three eggs into the bowl. Beat well to mix the ingredients, and add two teaspoons of vanilla extract and a tablespoon of coconut oil into the bowl. Stir well to mix.

Once the wet ingredients are properly mixed, pour the dry ingredients into the bowl. Stir well or use an electric mixer to combine the ingredients, and stir until there are no more lumps. Pour the zucchini into the batter, and add the raisins and almonds as well. Mix to distribute these ingredients.

Pour the batter into a greased baking pan, which should have a bit of butter along the bottom to help make the cake tasty. Put the pan into the oven, and let it cook for about 50 minutes. The cake will take longer to cook than your average flour cake, but you'll know that it's done when a toothpick or knife inserted into the center of the cake comes out clean.

Remove the cake from the oven, let cool for a few minutes, cut, and serve!

Apple Cobbler

Not quite the same as Apple Crumble, this Apple Cobbler recipe is the perfect grain-free breakfast treat! It will be crunchy, flavorful, and delightful, but it won't have any of the gluten that you're trying so hard to avoid.

Ingredients

For this dish, you will need:
6 apples
1 can of cranberry sauce
Brown sugar
1 cup of steel-cut oats
Cinnamon
Soy milk
Butter

Preparation:

To begin, peel and cut the apples. You will want to make them small slices, easy enough to fit into your mouth without being too small.

Preheat the oven to about 350 F once the apples are done. Grease a baking tray with a bit of butter, and set it aside as you move on.

Combine the apples and the cranberry sauce in a bowl, and add in 2 or 3 tablespoons of the brown sugar. Add ¼ cup of soy milk, and mix the ingredients well to ensure that they are properly combined.

Melt a bit of butter on the stove, and pour the butter over the top of the oats. Toss the oats to coat them evenly with the butter.

Place the apple mixture into the pan, and cover it with a top layer of oats. Place the pan into the oven, and let it cook for about 35 or 40 minutes. You'll see that the oats turn a pleasant golden brown, and the juices released by the apple and cranberry sauce will bubble nicely.

Remove from the oven, let cool for a few minutes, and serve as the perfect healthy breakfast!

Breakfast Cereal Sans Gluten

A healthy breakfast cereal can be the perfect thing to get your morning started the right way, as it will provide you with slow-burning carbs that will give you energy all day long. This breakfast cereal will be perfect, as it comes without grain and will give you that energy boost you need for the long day ahead.

Ingredients:

For this dish, you will need:
½ cup of quinoa
½ cup of buckwheat groats
1 cup of brown basmati rice
½ cup of millet
½ cup of flax seeds
½ cup of sesame seeds
½ cup of cornmeal
½ cup of amaranth

Preparation:

To begin, place the basmati rice into a blender or grinder, and grind until you have produced a coarse rice flour. Empty the rice into a bowl.

Grind or blend all of the other ingredients, and you will end up with a mixture of various flours -- none of which will be wheat or grain flour, of course.

To prepare the cereal, put 4 cups of water into a pan to boil on the stove. Once the water is boiling, add in about a cup of the cereal mixture and a pinch of salt. Add a tablespoon or two of milk powder, and let the ingredients cook until they have thickened.

To add some flavor, add in a bit of cinnamon, some butter, and a tablespoon of sugar. You'll find that these ingredients will sweeten the cereal, and a bit of milk will help to make it more edible.

The cereal mixture will take about 20 minutes to cook, and you should keep the heat low to prevent it from burning. After 20 minutes has passed, scoop into a bowl, let cool for a minute, and enjoy!

Rice Stuffing

Need to stuff that Thanksgiving turkey but don't want to use bread? This rice turkey or chicken stuffing will be the perfect thing for you! It's tasty, subtle, and easy to make, and it will enable you to give your turkey the right filling.

Ingredients:

For this dish, you will need:
2 cups of white rice
Water
Chicken bouillon
1 onion
Butter
Garlic
1 celery stalk
Parsley
Salt
Sage
Thyme
Pepper, to taste

Preparation:

To begin, you will need to dice the onions as fine as you

can. Make sure to chop the onions very small.

Place a pot on the stove to heat, and add about a tablespoon of butter into the bottom of the pan. Once the butter has melted, add the onions into the mixture. Let the onions fry for a minute, and chop the garlic as you do so. Add about 5 cloves of garlic -- chopped fine -- into the pan, and fry the garlic along with the onions.

Once the onions have begun to brown around the edges, add the uncooked rice into the pan. You will want to cook the rice until it shows signs of beginning to burn, and the grains will become slightly browned. At this point, add the 2 cups of water into the pan, and cover it.

Once the rice begins to simmer, add a tablespoon or two of chicken bouillon into the pan. Dice the celery stalk, and drop the pieces into the pan. Sprinkle parsley, salt, sage, thyme, and all the pepper you want into the rice.

The simmering water will cook the rice in about 20 minutes, but keep a close eye on it. once the level of the rice rises above the water level, you only have about 5 to 7 more minutes until the rice is completely cooked. Make sure the rice doesn't burn, and don't let it cook all the way. The rice should still be a bit crunchy when you turn it off.

Once the rice is cooked, remove it from the pan, let it cool, and use it to stuff your turkey. The partially cooked rice will finish cooking as the turkey cooks, and it will come out soft and fluffy!

Gluten Free Irish Shortbread

There's nothing like a good piece of Irish shortbread to eat after your Irish beef stew, and you'll find that a hearty piece of this bread will go down nicely. The best part about this bread: it's made without gluten or wheat!

Ingredients

For this dish, you will need:
2 cups of butter
2 cups of rye flour
1 cup of corn flour
2 cups of brown sugar

Preparation:

To begin, heat the oven to 300 degrees. Take the time to grease two baking pans, or use grease paper to prevent a mess.

Soften the butter in a double boiler, or leave it at room temperature for an hour to make it easier to mash. Use a fork to mix the sugar into the butter, and combine it until it is creamy and blended. Add the corn flour and the rye flour, and combine into a nice dough.

Divide the dough that you have into two portions, and press each portion of dough into the pans that you have prepared. Use the fork to prick some shallow holes, dividing the bread into individual portions. You can sprinkle a bit of sugar to make it decorative.

Place the baking pans into the oven, and let them cook for about an hour. You'll find that the bread can cook in as little time as 45 minutes, so keep an eye on it. You may notice that the edges of the bread are getting browned, and the top will be nicely golden.

Cut the bread into individual pieces while it is still warm, and enjoy!

Asian Sesame Noodles

If you love the taste of the Orient, this will definitely be the dish for you. These tasty noodles are grain-free, but they're absolutely delightful! With the right ingredients added to this dish, you'll have everything you need to get your Oriental on!

Ingredients

For this dish, you will need:
400 grams of Gluten-free noodles
Sesame oil
2 carrots
Garlic
Fresh ginger root
1 onion
½ head of cabbage
½ pepper
1 sprig of cilantro
Almond butter
Gluten-free soy sauce

Preparation:

To begin, you'll need to put a pot of water on the stove to boil. Add about 3 cups of water per 100 grams of noodles, and give it a few minutes to boil.

As the water is heating up, dice the ginger, garlic, and onions. You can use as much garlic as you want, but add no more than a teaspoon of fresh ginger root. Julienne the carrots, the bell pepper, and the cabbage, making the slices as thin as possible.

Place a wok on the stove to heat, and pour in a few tablespoons of sesame oil. Once the oil is hot, drop in the ginger, garlic, and onions. Stir fry the ingredients for a few minutes, and add in the carrots. Once the carrots have begun to soften, add in the peppers and the cabbage. Cook for just 3 minutes, and add the soy sauce into the mixture.

Place the noodles in the water to cook, and keep a close eye on them. You don't want them to overcook, as they'll be quite unpleasant. Make sure that they're al dente, and remove them from the stove. Drain the water, run cold water over the noodles, and throw the noodles into the wok.

Stir fry the noodles with the other ingredients, adding a tablespoon of almond butter, 2 tablespoons of soy sauce, and ½ tablespoon of sesame oil to flavor the noodles. Cook until the liquid has all been eliminated from the wok, leaving you with a dry, slightly fried noodle dish.

Serve the noodles onto two plates, chop the cilantro to sprinkle on top of the noodles, and serve with chopsticks and your favorite Chinese hot sauce.

Shrimp Cakes

Want to enjoy some seafood, but can't eat gluten? These gluten-free shrimp cakes are an absolute delight, and they'll help you to get a lot more protein in your diet. They're fairly easy to make, but they're definitely a delicious meal that will be ideal for anyone on a weight loss diet.

Ingredients

For this dish, you will need:
1 pound of shrimp
1 red bell pepper
2 cloves of garlic
Scallions
Lime juice
Sea salt
Chipotle
1 egg
½ cup of almond flour
Grapeseed or peanut
½ cup of chopped cilantro

Preparation:

To begin, peel and de-vein the shrimp. This can be a lengthy process, so be prepared to spend at least 20 minutes in this activity.

Once the shrimp has been prepared, throw them into the blender or food processor. Press the pulse button until the shrimp has been chopped fine, and remove the shrimp from the blender.

Pour the shrimp into a bowl, and add a teaspoon of sea salt, the cilantro, and ¼ teaspoon of chipotle. Crack the egg into the bowl, and mix it well to combine.

Dice the scallions, the garlic, and the bell pepper, making sure that they are very finely chopped. Add them into the bowl, and stir to mix properly. Add the lime juice for the finishing flavor touches.

Use your hands to form the ingredients into balls, which you will dip into the almond flour to coat them thoroughly as you flatten them into patties.

Place a skillet on the stove to heat, and add enough oil to fry the patties. Place four of the patties into the skillet at a time, and cook for about 5 minutes. Turn the patty onto its other side, and cook it until that side is also browned.

Remove the cooked patties from the pan, and place them on a paper towel to drain as you cook the rest. You should obtain about 12 patties from this mixture.

Enjoy with a simple marinara sauce, or just pour some of your favorite hot sauce over the patties to make them taste delicious!

Stuffed Bell Peppers

This dish is made with a rice stuffing that will be absolutely divine, not to mention free of gluten. If you want to enjoy a delicious stuffed bell pepper, this is a recipe that you must try!

Ingredients:

For this dish, you will need:
6 green bell peppers
Diced green chilies
1 pound of ground beef
1 onion
5 cloves of garlic
1 cup of rice
Cumin
Cilantro
Chili powder
Sea salt

Preparation:

To begin, place a pan on the stove to heat. Pour a tablespoon of oil into the bottom of the pan, and dice one of the cloves of garlic. Cook the garlic until it's nicely browned, and add the rice into the pan. Once the rice is toasted, pour 1 cup of water into the pan. Cover it and cook on low heat until the rice is done. Remove from the heat and set aside.

Dice the onion and the rest of the garlic very finely, and place a skillet on the stove to heat. With a bit of oil in the bottom of the pan, sauté the garlic and onions for a few minutes. Add the ground beef into the pan, and cook it until it's well done. Add ½ can of diced green chilies 3 minutes before the meat is done, and cook them with the meat. Once you have turned off the meat, add in a teaspoon of cumin, ½ cup of diced fresh cilantro, a teaspoon of chili powder, and a tablespoon of sea salt.

Take the ground beef mixture and add it into the pan with the rice. Mix well to combine, and add salt and pepper as desired.

Use a knife to score around the top of the bell pepper, and pull off the top to extract the seeds. Wash the peppers thoroughly to remove any remaining seeds.

Heat the oven to 350 F.

Use a spoon to scoop the rice and beef mixture into the bell peppers, stuffing them completely full. Remove the seeds from the tops of the bell peppers, and place the tops back on the peppers. Place the bell peppers on a tray, and place the tray in the oven.

Let the peppers cook for about 45 minutes to an hour, and they will be ready to eat!

Gluten-Free Turkey Club

This is a delicious sandwich that you can make all on your own, and you'll be able to use gluten-free bread to slap together this quick and easy meal. You can used gluten-free bread that you bought from the store, or you can make your own loaf of gluten-free nut bread. This recipe will just tell you how to make the perfect sandwich, but there's a recipe further down that will tell you how to make the bread.

Ingredients

For this dish, you will need:
3 slices of gluten-free bread
4 slices of turkey ham
1 avocado
2 slices of your favorite cheese
Onion
Tomato
Canned chipotle chili peppers
Lettuce
Pickles
Alfalfa sprouts
Dijon mustard
Tabasco sauce
Light mayonnaise

Preparation:

To begin, place a skillet on the stove to heat. Once the skillet is properly hot, place the bread on the skillet. Only toast one side of two slices of bread, but toast the third slice on both sides.

Remove the bread from the skillet, and start with one of the half-toasted slices placed toasted side down.

Onto this slice of bread, spread a bit of mayonnaise. Add 2 slices of turkey, one slice of cheese, 1 onion ring, two pickles, and the alfalfa sprouts. Sprinkle Tabasco sauce generously. Grab the fully toasted slice of bread, and spread Dijon mustard on one side and mayo on the other. Place the toast mustard side down on top of the other ingredients.

Add the last two slices of turkey onto the sandwich, along with the cheese, 1 slice of tomato, 1 diced canned chipotle pepper, 3 slices of avocado, and two leaves of lettuce. Sprinkle Tabasco sauce generously onto the sandwich, and spread Dijon mustard onto the untoasted side of the final piece of bread before completing your sandwich.

Cut in half, serve, and enjoy!

All Purpose, Gluten and Grain-Free Nut Bread

This is the nut bread that you can use to make sandwiches, cheese toast, eat with your morning coffee, or just snack on when you're hungry. It's a gluten and grain-free bread that you can use for just about anything, and it will be the perfect option regardless of what sweet or savory dish you need bread for. It's also quick and easy to make!

Ingredients:

For this dish, you will need:
¼ cup of flax meal
1 ½ cups of almond flour
Salt
4 eggs
½ teaspoon of baking soda
1 cup of walnuts, hazelnuts, almonds, and other nuts.
¼ cup of sesame seeds
¼ cup of amaranth
¼ cup of sunflower seeds
1 teaspoon of apple cider vinegar
1 teaspoon of agave honey

Preparation:

To begin, heat the oven to about 350 F, and grease two bread pans.

Combine the almond flour with the flax meal, baking soda, and a pinch of salt in a bowl, stirring well to ensure that the ingredients are properly combined.

Crack the eggs into a bowl, and use a fork or whisk to beat them well. Make sure they are frothy, and add into the bowl the agave honey and vinegar. Mix the wet and dry ingredients together in a bowl, and add the various nuts and seeds into the same bowl. Use a fork or whisk to mix the ingredients properly until there are no lumps.

Pour the bread batter into the greased bread pans, and put them in the oven. The bread will probably take about 30 to 40 minutes to cook, so keep an eye on them. Check the bread for doneness by inserting a knife into the center, and it will come out clean when it's done cooking.

Remove from the oven, set aside to cool, and slice the bread once it has reached room temperature. You now have the ideal loaf of bread for just about anything!

Pad Thai

Pad Thai is one of the most popular Thai dishes in the country, and it will be a wonderful grain-free alternative to the more popular Chinese and Japanese fried noodle dishes. It's fairly easy to make, and it's absolutely delicious!

Ingredients

For this dish, you will need:
6 ounces of rice noodles
Sesame oil
1 onion
1 head of broccoli
Water
4 cloves of garlic
Scallions
Cilantro
Peanuts
Salt and pepper, to taste

Preparation:

To begin, place a pot of water on the stove to boil. Bring the water to a boil, and drop the rice noodles in to cook. The package will usually have clear instructions on how to cook the noodles, so follow them precisely for al dente noodles. Drain the noodles, run cold water over them, and set them aside.

Place a skillet on the stove to heat, and add a bit of sesame oil into the bottom. Dice the onion very fine, and add it into the pan to be sautéed. Cook the onions on medium-low heat, and make sure they are nicely browned.

As the onions are cooking, cut the broccoli into bite-sized spears. Once about 10 minutes has passed, add the broccoli in with the browned onions. Add ¼ cup of water, and cover the pan. Let the broccoli sauté with the onions for roughly 5 minutes, after which time it will become soft and turn a bright color.

Add salt to the pan, and dice the garlic to be added as well. Add a bit more sesame oil to ensure that the ingredients don't dry out, and add some diced peanuts into the pan. Use a tablespoon of arrowroot powder and water to thicken the mixture, and stir fry the ingredients to ensure that the powder is spread all around.

Place the noodles onto a plate, and pour the vegetable mixture over the top. If you want to add some protein, throw some shrimp into a pan and grill them to serve on top of the vegetables and noodles.

Garnish with some scallions and diced cilantro, and enjoy!

Gluten-Free Chicken Noodle Soup

There's nothing like a cup of chicken noodle soup when you're feeling ill, but wheat noodles would just make the problem worse. With this grain-free chicken noodle soup, you'll always feel better, and it is a tasty soup that you can't help but love!

Ingredients:

For this dish, you will need:
1 liter of chicken broth
1 stalk of celery
1 onions
3 cloves of garlic
1 carrot
1 zucchini
1 pack of gluten-free noodles
½ chicken breast

Preparation:

To begin, dice the onions and the carrots very finely. Make sure that they are diced very small.

Place a pot on the stove to heat, and drop a tablespoon of olive oil into the bottom. Add the garlic and onions into the pot, and sauté them until they are browned.

Once the onions and garlic are properly cooked, add the chicken broth into the pot. Set the heat on medium, and let the broth boil.

As the broth is heating up, cut the carrots into small pieces about as large as your fingernails. Throw them into the pot, along with the celery - which you will slice into small pieces as well.

Run the zucchini through a julienne slicer, and you'll have what looks like simple noodles. Put them into the pot, and let them cook along with the other ingredients.

On the side, add a bit of butter into a skillet. Slice the chicken breast into small chunks, and cook the chicken in the pot until browned on the outside. Add the partially cooked chicken into the pot of soup, ensuring that you get all the liquid and oil from the skillet.

Turn the soup up to high heat, and let it cook for another 15 minutes. Once that time has passed, drop the gluten-free soup noodles into the mixture, and let them cook on low heat. Once the noodles have cooked properly, turn off the fire and remove the pot from the stove.

Serve, add a splash of lime, and enjoy!

Gluten-Free Potato Beef Stew

Want to make a thick, hearty stew without adding flour or wheat to the mixture? This delicious stew will be an ideal meal to have on a cold winter evening, and it will be just as rich and hearty as any stew made with flour to thicken it!

Ingredients:

For this dish, you will need:
4 potatoes
1 pound of stew meat
2 carrots
1 onion
5 cloves of garlic
½ cup of table wine
¼ cup of soy sauce
1 cup of milk
2 liters of beef broth
Salt and pepper, to taste
Preparations:

To begin, peel one potato, dice it, and place it in a small pot of water to boil. Let the potato cook for about an hour, adding more water into the pot whenever necessary. Once the potato has cooked for the prescribed 60 minutes, drain all but the final dregs of water, mash with a fork, and set aside.

Place a soup pot on the stove to heat, along with a couple of tablespoons of peanut oil in the bottom of the pot.

Dice the onion and the garlic, and add them into the pot to sauté. Add the onions first, and let them cook until nearly browned before adding in the garlic.

Dice the stew meat into small bite-sized pieces, and add them into the pot once the garlic has been properly cooked. Cook the meat until it has been browned on the outside, and add the beef broth into the pot. Bring the beef broth to a boil as you cut the other vegetables.

Cut the potatoes into medium-sized cubes, and add them into the pot. Peel and cut the potatoes into slices, and add them into the pot.

Let the stew boil for about 20 minutes, or until you're sure the potatoes are nearly cooked. Add in the soy sauce, table wine, and the milk, and let it keep cooking. Add salt and pepper as desired, along with crushed bay leaves for added flavor.

Just 5 minutes before you are about to turn the soup off, add in the mashed potato. Stir the soup well, ensuring that the mashed potato is diluted properly. The starch from the potato will thicken the stew, but it will ensure that the other ingredients aren't overcooked.

Serve with nut bread, and enjoy!

Grain-Free Ideal Breakfast

The ideal way to start the day is with a rich breakfast, but the average breakfast consists of grain-laden toast, pancakes, or other things that are made with grain. If you want the perfect breakfast without adding grain to your diet, this is the recipe for you!

Ingredients:

For this dish, you will need:
3 eggs
2 slices of turkey or Canadian bacon
6 oranges
2 Slices of Nut bread (see recipe above)
Butter
Honey
Coffee

Preparation:

To begin, place a skillet on the stove to heat. Once the skillet is hot, add the bacon and cook until done. Remove the bacon from the stove, and place on a paper towel to drain.

Leaving the bacon grease in the bottom of the pan, let it

reheat until ready for the eggs. Crack one egg into the pan, and crack the other two eggs into a cup -- making sure to get only the egg whites. Add the two egg whites into the pan, and cook the eggs until done as desired. (If you don't like your eggs to be liquid on the top, flip them over and let them sit in the pan for 3 seconds before scooping them onto your plate.)

Add the slices of nut bread onto the plate, along with the Canadian or turkey bacon. Spread butter and honey as desired on the bread, and serve yourself a cup of coffee.

Squeeze the oranges, and enjoy your fresh cup of OJ for the ideal grain-free breakfast!

Dark Chicken Soup

If you're not too particular about the way your soup looks, you'll find that this will be the ideal meal for you! It comes loaded with all the nutrients you need, and there are even a few noodles floating around to help fill you up. All in all, however, it's a nicely low calorie meal - and grain-free as well!

Ingredients

For this dish, you will need:

2 liters of chicken broth

1 bunch of chard

2 carrots

1 bunch of spinach

1 cup of shitake mushrooms

1 pack of shitake mushroom noodles

¼ pound of chicken breast

Preparation:

To begin, place the chard and spinach in a pot with 2 cups of water and 2 cups of chicken stock. Bring the veggies to a boil, and let them cook until they are soft. Pour the soup into the food processor, blend it until it is completely liquefied, and set it aside.

Pour the chicken broth into a pot, and bring it to a boil. Cut the carrots and shitake mushrooms into slices, and add them into the soup. Pour the liquefied dark greens into the pot, and let them cook along with the chicken broth.

In a pan on the side, add a pat of butter into the bottom as the pan heats. Dice the chicken breast into chunks, and let the breast cook until it is browned on the outside. Once it is nearly cooked, pour the chicken and the grease into the soup pot. Let it cook until you're sure the chicken is thoroughly done.

Add the mushroom noodles a few minutes before you want to cook the soup, and follow the cooking instructions on the package. The noodles shouldn't take too long to cook, and you can serve out the soup while it's still piping hot!

Carrot Muffins

These delicious muffins will help you to start the day out right, and you can munch on a couple of them as you head to work. Thanks to the fact that they're completely grain-free, they'll be the perfect option for you!

Ingredients

For this dish, you will need:
¼ teaspoon of baking soda
¼ cup of coconut flour
Cinnamon
3 eggs
Salt
¼ cup of oil
¼ cup of natural molasses
Vanilla
3 carrots
¼ cup of raspberries, blackberries, and black currants

Preparation:

To begin, preheat the oven to about 350 F. This is the perfect temperature for muffins, as it will keep cooking time down without risking burning the muffins.

Combine the baking soda, coconut flour, and a teaspoon of cinnamon in a bowl, and stir it well to ensure that it's properly combined.

In a separate bowl, crack and mix the eggs. Whip them until they are frothy, and pour the oil, molasses, and a teaspoon of vanilla into the mix. Beat well, add a pinch of salt, and combine the wet ingredients with the dry.

Use a whisk to combine the wet and dry ingredients well, and stir until you are sure there are no lumps.

With a bit of butter, grease a muffin tray. You'll get about 12 to 18 medium-sized muffins, though as many as 30 mini muffins. Put the tray into the oven, and cook the muffins for about 30 minutes. Insert a knife into the top of one muffin, and it should come out clean once it's done.

Remove the muffins from the oven, scoop them out of their tray, and set them aside to cool.

Almond and Grilled Chicken Salad

The beauty of salads is that they are some of the best grain-free recipes, and you won't have to worry about getting gluten if you eat a healthy salad. If you want to really go all out with the salad, add nuts and lots of filling veggies! You'll find that it will be tasty and very enjoyable!

Ingredients:

For this dish, you will need:
1 pound of chicken breast
1 head of Romaine or Iceberg lettuce
1 cup of raw almonds
1 cup of raw peanuts
1 cup of dried cranberries
1 apple
½ cup of olive oil
½ cup of apple cider vinegar
1 cup of gluten-free soy sauce
Salt
Sesame seeds

Preparation:

To begin, slice the chicken breast into steaks about ¾ inch thick. You'll get about 3 steaks from a single chicken breast. Place the chicken breast on a grill, and rub a seasoning of salt, pepper, garlic, and Parmesan cheese onto the breast before cooking it. Grill the chicken well on both sides, and make sure that the middle of the chicken is cooked before removing it from the grill. Set the chicken aside.

Soak the lettuce in a bowl of ice cold water, which will make it crunchy and crispy. Once the lettuce has soaked for 30 minutes, use your hands to rip it into bite-sized leaves.

Slice the apple into quarters, cut out the cores, and cut the apple into small chunks. Add the apples into the salad, along with the cranberries.

In a skillet on the stove, place the almonds and peanuts together. The raw nuts will need to be toasted, and they will take about 20 minutes. Make sure to stir them every 5 minutes or so, and keep the heat on medium high to prevent them from burning. Once the almonds and peanuts are toasted, add them into the salad.

Slice the chicken breast into strips, and add them into the salad as well.

Combine the vinegar, soy sauce, and olive oil together, along with a pinch of salt and some black pepper. Pour this mixture over the salad, and sprinkle sesame seeds liberally on top to garnish the salad. It's now ready for you to eat!

Gluten-Free Breakfast Biscuits

There's nothing like a delicious, buttery biscuit to start your day off on the right foot, and these grain-free biscuits will be just what you need to enjoy your morning. They're easy to whip up, and you can take them with you to snack in your car on the way to work.

Ingredients

For this dish, you will need:
2 cups of almond flour
½ teaspoon of baking soda
2 eggs
1 teaspoon of honey
1/3 cup of butter or margarine
Salt

Preparation:

To begin, preheat the oven to about 350 F. This is the temperature that will allow the biscuits to turn golden brown on the outside, but without making the center of the biscuits too dry.

In a bowl, combine the almond flour with the baking soda and a pinch of salt. Stir well to ensure that there are no clumps of baking soda.

In another bowl, crack the eggs and beat them until they are frothy. Add in the butter and the honey, and beat well. You'll want to keep stirring until you have a slightly creamy mixture.

Fold the wet ingredients gently into the dry ones, and mix until you're sure that there are no lumps. You will need to keep stirring as the dough is formed.

Use a piece of greased baking paper to roll the biscuit dough out, and keep rolling until you've flattened the dough to about 1 ½ inches thick. Use a jar with a wide mouth to cut out the biscuits, and keep rolling the dough until you have turned it all into biscuits.

Transfer the biscuits to an oven tray with a piece of greased baking paper, and put the tray into the oven. Let the biscuits cook for about 15 minutes, and keep a close eye on them. You'll notice that the rounded edges of the biscuits will start to brown, and don't let them get too dark before removing them from the oven.

Use a spatula to scrape the biscuits off the greased baking sheet, and set them on a rack to cool. Once they're cool, spread a bit of butter and honey on them, and enjoy!

Nutty Granola

Granola is one of the best breakfasts that you can have, and you'll find that this nutty granola will be just the thing to stoke up your internal furnace first thing in the morning. It's a grain-free breakfast that will kick off your day in style!

Ingredients

For this dish, you will need:
1 cup of steel cut oats
2 cups of almonds
1 cup of amaranth
1 cup of raisins
1 cup of walnuts
1 tablespoon of vanilla
Butter
Cinnamon
Sugar

Preparation:

To begin, place a skillet on the stove to heat. Melt a cup of butter in the bottom of the skillet, and add the oats in once the butter is liquefied completely.

Use a spatula or wooden spoon to roll the oats thoroughly in the butter, and ensure that the oats are properly coated. Remove the skillet from the heat, and transfer the oats into a flat baking tray.

Preheat the oven to 350 F.

Add the raisins into the oats, and cut the almonds and walnuts in half. Add in the amaranth, and sprinkle a bit of sugar, cinnamon, and a few tablespoons of vanilla extract onto the oats. Make sure that the oats are mixed properly, and put the tray into the oven to cook.

Give the oats about 30 minutes to cook at 350 F, but keep checking them to ensure that they don't burn. You'll find that they'll become nice and crunchy once they've cooked properly, but let them cool down before eating them.

Grain-Free Breakfast Bars

Need something quick to munch on as you drive to work in the morning? Don't let the heavy traffic get you down, but make these delicious breakfast bars to help keep your mind off the fact that you're sitting and doing nothing. They're a healthy breakfast that you can enjoy on the go!

Ingredients

For this dish, you will need:
2 cups of almond flour
1/3 teaspoon of baking soda
1/3 cup of grapeseed oil
Vanilla extract
1/3 cup of honey
½ cup of shredded coconut
1/3 cup of raisins
1/3 cup of nuts (your preference)
¼ cup of flax seeds
¼ cup of amaranth
¼ pumpkin seeds

Preparation:

To begin, preheat the oven to 350 F.

In a bowl, combine the almond flour with a pinch of salt and the baking soda. Make sure to mix well, as that will eliminate any lumps of baking soda.

In another bowl, mix the honey with a tablespoon of vanilla and the grapeseed oil. The oil will be a bit hard to mix in, but a bit of effort will yield a properly mixed liquid.

Pour the wet ingredients in with the dry ones, and whisk vigorously to ensure that the wet and dry ingredients combine nicely without any lumps.

Once you're done mixing, add the nuts, seeds, raisins, coconut, and amaranth into the batter. Mix well to distribute the latest additions.

Use a bit of butter to grease the bottom of a baking tray, and pour the mixture into the pan. Place the pan in the oven, and let it cook for about 20 minutes at 350 F. You'll find that it turns a nice golden brown, and it will become very crunchy and a bit hard to cut.

Slice the bars into small pieces, and serve or set aside to eat on the go.

Garden-Style Hot Dogs

Hot dogs are one of the most popular American foods around, but the problem is the hot dog bun. If you want to enjoy a classic hot dog in a very unique way, these garden-style hot dogs will be an ideal way for you to eliminate the gluten from your meal.

Ingredients:

For this dish, you will need:
6 hot dogs
6 slices of bacon
1 head of Romaine lettuce
½ tomato
½ onion
Pickle relish
Sauerkraut
Ketchup
Mayo
Mustard
Tabasco sauce

Preparation:

To begin, soak the head of lettuce in ice cold water. The cold water will help to make the lettuce crunchier and crispier, which will make it much easier to eat.

Place a skillet on the stove, and let it heat. As the pan is heating, wrap one strip of bacon around each hotdog. You can hold the bacon in place using toothpicks, but make sure that the toothpicks don't interfere with the cooking process.

Let the hot dogs cook for about 20 minutes on low heat, and turn them regularly to ensure that they don't burn. The grease from the bacon will make them very tasty.

Once they're thoroughly cooked, remove the skillet from the stove, but leave the hot dogs inside.

Remove 12 strips of lettuce, and make 6 stacks of two leaves. Dice the tomato and the onions, making sure that they are very small.

Place a bit of sauerkraut in **the bottom** layer of lettuce, and stack the second leaf on top. Place each hot dog into the top leaf, and add tomato, onion, and pickle relish on top. Add the condiments of your choice, and enjoy the delicious, all-natural hot dog meal!

Grain-Free Mac and Cheese

Mac and Cheese is the quintessential American meal, but egg noodles are made with wheat. Using gluten-free noodles will allow you to still enjoy this delicious dish, but without having to worry about adding grain to your meal!

Ingredients

For this dish, you will need:
2 packs of gluten-free noodles
3 cups of grated cheddar cheese
½ cup of butter
1 ½ cups of milk
2 tablespoons of heavy cream
¼ pound of bacon
1 onion
4 cloves of garlic

Preparation:

To begin, place a skillet on the stove to heat. Add a bit of butter into the bottom of the skillet, and dice the onions as the pan gets hot. Add the onions into the bottom of the pan to sauté, and dice the garlic to add in once the onions begin to brown.

Remove the garlic and onions from the stove once the aroma of the garlic is extracted, and slice the bacon as the skillet heats up once again. Place a pot of water on the stove to boil, which will be for the noodles.

Once the skillet is hot, add the bacon into the pan. Cook until it is nicely browned, and remove from the stove.

Place the onions and garlic back on the stove, and pour the milk and bacon into the pan. Once the milk gets hot, add in the heavy cream and the butter. Bring the ingredients to a boil, and add the cheddar cheese into the mix. Turn the fire off, but leave the pan on the stove.

Boil the noodles, and cook them until they are al dente. Place the noodles back into the pot they were cooked in, add the cheese sauce over the top, garnish with a bit more cheese, and serve while hot!

Almond Raisin Muffins

These muffins are simple and easy to make, but they'll be delicious without a doubt! You can even top them with icing to make delicious cupcakes, or keep them light if you're on a diet! Enjoy them no matter where you are, as they are fantastic.

Ingredients:

For this dish, you will need:
1 cup of flax meal
1 cup of almond flour
1 tablespoon of baking powder
Nutmeg
Cinnamon
½ cup of raisins
1/3 cup of toasted **almonds**
1 stick of butter
Salt
4 eggs
½ cup of sugar
½ cup of buttermilk
2 tablespoons of brown sugar

Preparation:

To begin, you will need to heat the oven to about 375 F. Once the oven is hot, turn it down to 350 F, which is the ideal temperature for baking the muffins.

Combine the baking powder, flax meal, almond flour, and a pinch of salt in a bowl, mixing well to combine. Add a teaspoon each of cinnamon and nutmeg, and stir well.

Combine the butter, eggs, sugar, and milk in a bowl, and beat until the eggs are frothy and the butter is creamy. Using melted butter will make the process a lot quicker, but you can use an egg beater if you don't want to take the time to melt the butter.

Combine the wet and dry ingredients, and mix them well to eliminate any lumps. Add the raisins into the mix. Chop the toasted almonds into small pieces, and add them into the muffin batter as well.

Once the ingredients are all stirred in well, pour the muffin batter into a muffin baking tray. Use paper muffin cups if you want to limit the mess.

Place the muffins in the oven, and let them cook for

roughly 15 to 20 minutes, depending the altitude of your city(it takes longer for things to bake the higher above sea level you are). Insert a toothpick into the top of the muffins when they look cooked, and they are done when the toothpick comes out clean.

Remove the muffins from the tray, set them aside to cool, and serve.

Grain-Free Pizza

Pizza is one of the most popular dishes in the world, but it's hard to make a good pizza without using flour. This pizza is made without wheat, and it's a tasty alternative that gluten-sensitive people can enjoy without worrying about their stomachs acting up.

Ingredients

For this dish, you will need:

1 cup of quinoa flour
1 cup of potato flour
1 cup of almond flour
1 cup of buckwheat
Salt
Xanthan gum
4 teaspoons of dried yeast
Canola or olive oil
Water
Tomato sauce
Cheese
Pizza toppings of your choice

Preparation:

To begin, heat the oven to a toasty 350 F.

Grease some baking sheets with a bit of olive or canola oil, and place them on the trays where you will be cooking your pizza.

Sift the various flours, salt, and baking soda into a bowl, and combine the dry ingredients well. Add the yeast into the mixture.

Mix half a liter of warm water with a couple of tablespoons of olive oil, and add the wet ingredients into the dry ones. Mix the dough until it is properly combined, and set it aside for a few minutes to rise.

Once it has risen, use a spoon to scoop it into your pizza tray. Make a nicely rounded pizza, and put it in the oven to cook until the crust is golden brown.

All that is left to do is to scoop the pizza or tomato sauce onto the top of the crust, add cheese, and top with the ingredients of your choice. Put the crust back into the oven, and cook it until the cheese has properly melted.

Slice, serve, and enjoy!

Your Grain Free Meal Plan

So, you've got all these awesome grain-free recipes to work with! Whether you're trying to lose weight or just stay healthy, eating these foods will help you to keep grain and gluten out of your life. If you want to add these delicious meals to your diet, here is an 11-day meal plan that you can use to incorporate all of these recipes into your life:

Day 1:
Breakfast: Buckwheat Pancakes
Lunch: Eggs and Nut Bread Toast
Dinner: Pad Thai

Day 2:
Breakfast: Gluten Free Waffles
Lunch: Grain-Free Cornbread with Grilled Chicken or Steak, plus plenty of veggies
Dinner: Special K cereal (made with rice rather than wheat flour)

Day 3:
Breakfast: Special K Cereal
Lunch: Stuffed Bell Peppers
Dinner: Chicken with Rice Stuffing

Dessert: Roasted Almond Cookies

Day 4:
Breakfast: Apple Cobbler
Lunch: Asian Sesame Noodles
Dinner: Almond and Grilled Chicken Salad

Day 5:
Breakfast: Breakfast Cereal Sans Gluten
Lunch: Grain Free Breaded Chicken with Nut Bread and veggies
Dinner: Gluten-Free Chicken Noodle Soup with Nut Bread
Dessert: Gluten and Sugar-Free Gingerbread Cake

Day 6:
Breakfast: Carrot Muffins
Lunch: Gluten-Free Turkey Club
Dinner: Curried Quinoa with Chick Peas

Day 7:
Breakfast: Grain-Free Ideal Breakfast
Lunch: Dark Chicken Soup with Nut Bread
Dinner: Grain-Free Mac and Cheese

Day 8:
Breakfast: Gluten-Free Breakfast Biscuits

Lunch: Gluten-Free Potato Beef Stew

Dinner: Shrimp Cakes

Dessert: Gluten-Free Irish Shortbread

Day 9:

Breakfast: Nutty Granola

Lunch: Dark Chicken Soup with Nut Bread

Dinner: Special K Cereal

Day 10:

Breakfast: Breakfast Bars

Lunch: Garden-Style Hot Dogs

Dinner: Sesame Seed Chicken Fried Steak

Day 11:

Breakfast: Almond Flour Muffins

Lunch: Grain-Free Pizza

Dinner: Special K Cereal

The meal plan above doesn't come with the calorie count on each food item, but that's something that won't be as important as the fact that they are all grain-free foods. You can eat them without worrying too much about calories, but try and keep the consumption of these foods to a healthy minimum in order to avoid gaining weight!

All of these recipes can be found online, though some of them are our own original creations. You can probably find similar recipes on websites like AllRecpes.com, About.com, and particularly ElanasPantry.com. They are all recipes that someone made, and we just wanted to share them with you. We've made a few adjustments to the various recipes so that you'll get only our unique grain-free flavor on the recipes, but you'll find that there are many like them. The important thing is that you can enjoy your grain-free cooking and eating, and we wanted to provide you with a recipe book that you can use to prepare delicious meals free of grain and gluten. We apologize if you've seen these recipes elsewhere, and we hope that you enjoy the creations we have presented to you!

[1] http://www.stuff.co.nz/life-style/38883/The-effects-of-gluten-on-health